Sophie May

Captain Horace

Sophie May

Captain Horace

ISBN/EAN: 9783337082741

Printed in Europe, USA, Canada, Australia, Japan

Cover: Foto ©ninafisch / pixelio.de

More available books at **www.hansebooks.com**

SOPHIE MAY'S

LITTLE FOLKS' BOOKS.

Any volume sold separately.

DOTTY DIMPLE SERIES. — Six volumes. Illustrated. Per volume, 75 cents.

Dotty Dimple at her Grandmother's.
Dotty Dimple at Home.
Dotty Dimple out West.
Dotty Dimple at Play.
Dotty Dimple at School.
Dotty Dimple's Flyaway.

FLAXIE FRIZZLE STORIES. — Six volumes. Illustrated. Per volume, 75 cents.

Flaxie Frizzle.	Little Pitchers.	Flaxie's Kittyleen.
Doctor Papa.	The Twin Cousins.	Flaxie Growing Up.

LITTLE PRUDY STORIES. — Six volumes. Handsomely Illustrated. Per volume, 75 cents.

Little Prudy.
Little Prudy's Sister Susy.
Little Prudy's Captain Horace.
Little Prudy's Story Book.
Little Prudy's Cousin Grace.
Little Prudy's Dotty Dimple.

LITTLE PRUDY'S FLYAWAY SERIES. — Six volumes. Illustrated. Per volume, 75 cents.

Little Folks Astray.	Little Grandmother.
Prudy Keeping House.	Little Grandfather.
Aunt Madge's Story.	Miss Thistledown.

LEE AND SHEPARD, PUBLISHERS,

BOSTON.

Captain Horace.

LITTLE PRUDY STORIES

STORIES

BY SOPHIE MAY

ILLUSTRATED

LITTLE PRUDY'S CAPTAIN HORACE

LEE & SHEPARD BOSTON

LITTLE PRUDY SERIES.

CAPTAIN HORACE.

BY

SOPHIE MAY.

BOSTON 1894
LEE AND SHEPARD PUBLISHERS
10 MILK STREET NEXT " THE OLD SOUTH MEETING HOUSE "

TO

MY LITTLE NEPHEW

WILLY WHEELER.

FROM HIS AFFECTIONATE

AUNT.

PREFACE.

You wide-awake little boys, who make whistles of willow, and go fishing and training, — Horace is very much like you, I suppose. He is by no means perfect, but he is brave and kind, and scorns a lie. I hope you and he will shake hands and be friends.

(b)

CONTENTS.

(6)

CAPTAIN HORACE.

———

CHAPTER I.

MAKING CANDY.

GRACE and Horace Clifford lived in Indiana, and so were called "Hoosiers."

Their home, with its charming grounds, was a little way out of town, and from the front windows of the house you could look out on the broad Ohio, a river which would be very beautiful, if its yellow waters were only once settled. As far as the eye could see, the earth was one vast plain, and, in order to touch it, the sky seemed to stoop very low; whereas, in New England, the gray-headed mountains appear to go up part way to meet the sky. (5)

One fine evening in May, brown-eyed Horace and blue-eyed Grace stood on the balcony, leaning against the iron railing, watching the stars, and chatting together.

One thing is very sure : they never dreamed that from this evening their sayings and doings — particularly Horace's — were to be printed in a book. If any one had whispered such a thing, how dumb Horace would have grown, his chin snuggling down into a hollow place in his neck ! and how nervously Grace would have laughed ! walking about very fast, and saying, —

"O, it's too bad, to put Horace and me in a book ! I say it's too bad ! Tell them to wait till my hair is curled, and I have my new pink dress on ! And tell them to make Horace talk better ! He plays so much with the Dutch boys. O, Horace isn't fit to print !"

This is what she might have said if she had thought of being "put in a book;" but as she knew nothing at all about it, she only stood very quietly leaning against the balcony-railing, and looking up at the evening sky, merry with stars.

"What a shiny night, Horace! What do the stars look like? Is it diamond rings?"

"I'll tell you, Gracie; it's cigars they look like — just the ends of cigars when somebody is smoking."

At that moment the cluster called the "Seven Sisters" was drowned in a soft, white cloud.

"Look," said Grace; "there are some little twinkles gone to sleep, all tucked up in a coverlet. I don't see what makes you think of dirty cigars! They look to me like little specks of gold harps ever so far off, so you can't hear the music. O, Horace, don't you want to be an angel, and play on a beautiful harp?"

"I don't know," said her brother, knitting his brows, and thinking a moment; "when I can't live any longer, you know, then I'd like to go up to heaven; but now, I'd a heap sooner be a *soldier!*"

"O, Horace, you'd ought to rather be an angel! Besides, you're too little for a soldier!"

"But I grow. Just look at my hands; they're bigger than yours, this minute!"

"Why, Horace Clifford, what makes them so black?"

"O, *that's* no account! I did it climbin' trees. Barby tried to scour it off, but it sticks. I don't care — soldiers' hands ain't white, are they, Pincher?"

The pretty dog at Horace's feet shook his ears, meaning to say, —

"I should think not, little master; soldiers have very dirty hands, if you say so."

"Come," said Grace, who was tired of gazing at the far-off star-land; "let's go down and see if Barbara hasn't made that candy: she said she'd be ready in half an hour."

They went into the library, which opened upon the balcony, through the passage, down the front stairs, and into the kitchen, Pincher following close at their heels.

It was a very tidy kitchen, whose white floor was scoured every day with a scrubbing-brush. Bright tin pans were shining upon the walls, and in one corner stood a highly polished cooking-stove, over which Barbara Kinckle, a rosy-cheeked German girl, was stooping to watch a kettle of boiling molasses. Every now and then she raised the spoon with which she was stirring it, and let the half-made candy drip back into the kettle in ropy streams. It looked very tempting, and gave out a delicious odor. Perhaps it was not strange that the children thought they were kept waiting a long while.

"Look here, Grace," muttered Horace, loud enough for Barbara to hear; "don't you think she's just the slowest kind?"

"It'll sugar off," said Grace, calmly, as if she had made up her mind for the worst; "don't you know how it sugared off once when ma was making it, and let the fire go 'most out'?"

"Now just hear them childers," said good-natured Barbara; "where's the little boy and girl that wasn't to speak to me one word, if I biled 'em some candies?"

"There, now, Barby, I wasn't speaking to you," said Horace; "I mean I wasn't talking to *her*, Grace. Look here: I've heard you spell, but you didn't ask me my Joggerphy."

"*Geography*, you mean, Horace."

"Well, Ge-ography, then. Here's the book: we begin at the Mohammedans."

Horace could pronounce that long name very well, though he had no idea what it meant. He knew there was a book called the Koran, and would have told you Mr. Mohammed wrote it; but so had Mr. Colburn written an Arithmetic, and whether both these gentlemen were alive, or both dead, was more than he could say.

"Hold up your head," said Grace, with dignity, and looking as much as possible like tall Miss Allen, her teacher. "Please repeat your verse."

The first sentence read, "They consider Moses and Christ as true prophets, but Mohammed as the greatest and last.'

"I'll tell you," said Horace : "they think that Christ and Moses was good enough prophets, but Mohammed was a heap better."

"Why, Horace, it doesn't say any such think in the book! It begins, '*They consider.*'"

"I don't care," said the boy, "Miss Jordan tells us to get the sense of it. Ma, musn't I get the sense of it?" he added, as Mrs. Clifford entered the kitchen.

"But, mamma," broke in Grace, eagerly, "our teacher wants us to commit the verses : she says a great deal about committing the verses."

"If you would give me time to answer," said Mrs. Clifford, smiling, "I should say both your teachers are quite right. You should 'get the sense of it,' as Horace says, and after that commit the verses."

"But, ma, do you think Horace should say 'heap,' and 'no account,' and such words?"

"It would certainly please me," said Mrs. Clifford, "if he would try to speak more correctly. My little boy knows how much I dislike some of his expressions."

"There, Horace," cried Grace, triumphantly, "I always said you talked just like the Dutch boys; and it's very, **very** improper!"

But just then it became evident that the molasses was boiled enough, for Barbara poured it into a large buttered platter, and set it out of doors to cool. After this, the children could do nothing but watch the candy till it was ready to pull.

Then there was quite a bustle to find an apron for Horace, and to make sure that his little stained hands were "spandy clean,"

and " fluffed " all over with flour, from his
wrists to the tips of his fingers.   Grace
said she wished it wasn't so much trouble
to attend to boys; and, after all, Horace
only pulled a small piece of the candy, and
dropped half of that on the nice white floor.

Barbara did the most of the pulling.   She
was quite a sculptor when she had plastic
candy in her hands.   Some of it she cut
into sticks, and some she twisted into curious images, supposed to be boys and girls,
horses and sheep.

After Grace and Horace had eaten several
of the " boys and girls," to say nothing of
" handled baskets," and " gentlemen's slippers," Barbara thought it high time they
were " sound abed and asleep."

So now, as they go up stairs, we will
wish them a good night and pleasant
dreams.

CHAPTER II.

CAMPING OUT.

"WHAT is the matter with my little son?" said Mr. Clifford, one morning at breakfast; for Horace sat up very stiffly in his chair, and refused both eggs and muffins, choosing instead a slice of dry toast and a glass of water.

"Are you sick, Horace?" asked his mother, tenderly.

"No, ma'am," replied the boy, blushing; "but I want to get to be a soldier!"

Mr. Clifford and his wife looked at each other across the table, and smiled.

"O, papa," said Grace, "I shouldn't want

2

to be a soldier if I couldn't have anything nice to eat. Can't they get pies and canned peaches and things? Will they go without buckwheat cakes and sirup in the winter?"

"Ah! my little daughter, men who love their country are willing to make greater sacrifices than merely nice food."

Horace put on one of his lofty looks, for he somehow felt that his father was praising *him*.

"Pa," said Grace, "please tell me what's a sacrifice, anyhow?"

"A sacrifice, my daughter, is the giving up of a dear or pleasant thing for the sake of duty: that is very nearly what it means. For instance, if your mamma consents to let me go to the war, because she thinks I ought to go, she will make what is called a sacrifice."

"Do not let us speak of it now, Henry," said Mrs. Clifford, looking quite pale.

"O, my dear papa," cried Grace, bursting into tears, "we couldn't live if you went to the war!"

Horace looked at the acorn on the lid of the coffee-urn, but said nothing. It cost his little heart a pang even to think of parting from his beloved father; but then wouldn't it be a glorious thing to hear him called General Clifford? And if he should really go away, wasn't it likely that the oldest boy, Horace, would take his place at the head of the table?

Yes, they should miss papa terribly; but he would only stay away till he "got a general;" and for that little while it would be pleasant for Horace to sit in the arm-chair and help the others to the butter, the toast, and the meat.

"Horace," said Mr. Clifford, smiling, "it will be some years before you can be a soldier: why do you begin now to eat dry bread?"

" I want to get used to it, sir."

" That indeed!" said Mr. Clifford, with a good-natured laugh, which made Horace wince a little. "But the eating of dry bread is only a small part of the soldier's tough times, my boy. Soldiers have to sleep on the hard ground, with knapsacks for pillows ; they have to march, through wet and dry, with heavy muskets, which make their arms ache."

"Look here, Barby," said Horace, that evening ; "I want a knapsack, to learn to be a soldier with. If I have ' tough times' now, I'll get used to it. Can't you find m carpet-bag, Barby ? "

"Carpet-bag? And what for a thing is that?" said Barbara, rousing from a nap, and beginning to click her knitting-needles.

'Here I was asleep again. Now, if I did keep working in the kitchen, I could sit up just what time I wants to; but when I sits down, I goes to sleep right off.''

And Barbara went on knitting, putting the yarn over the needle with her left hand, after the German fashion.

"But the carpet-bag, Barby: there's a black one 'some place,' in the trunk-closet or up-attic. Now, Barby, you know I helped pick those quails yesterday."

"Yes, yes, dear, when I gets my eyes open."

"I would sleep out doors, but ma says I'd get cold; so I'll lie on the floor in the bathing-room. O, Barby, I'll sleep like a trooper!"

But Horace was a little mistaken. A hard, unyielding floor makes a poor bed; and when, at the same time, one's neck is almost put out of joint by a carpet-bag stuffed with newspaper, it is not easy to go to sleep.

In a short time the little boy began to feel tired of "camping out;" and I am sorry to say that he employed some of the moonlight hours in studying the workmanship of his mother's watch, which had been left, by accident, hanging on a nail in the bathing-room.

He felt very guilty all the while; and when, at last, a *chirr-chirr* from the watch told that mischief had been done, his heart gave a quick throb of fright, and he stole off to his chamber, undressed, and went to bed in the dark.

Next morning he did not awake as early as usual, and, to his great dismay, came very near being late to breakfast.

"Good morning, little buzzard-lark," said

MR. CLIFFORD AND HIS SON.   *Page 27.*

his sister, coming into his room just as he was thrusting his arms into his jacket.

"Ho, Gracie! why didn't you wake me up?"

"I spoke to you seven times, Horace."

"Well, why didn't you pinch me, or shake me awake, or something?"

"Why, Horace, then you'd have been cross, and said, 'Gracie Clifford, let me alone!' You know you would, Horace."

The little boy stood by the looking-glass finishing his toilet, and made no reply.

"Don't you mean to behave?" said he, talking to his hair. "There, now, you've parted in the middle! Do you 'spose I'm going to look like a girl? Part the way you ought to, and lie down smooth! We'll see which will beat!"

"Why, what in the world is this?" exclaimed Grace, as something heavy dropped at her feet.

It was her mother's watch, which had fallen out of Horace's pocket.

"Where did you get this watch?"

No answer.

"Why, Horace, it doesn't tick: have you been playing with it?"

Still no answer.

"Now, that's just like you, Horace, to shut your mouth right up tight, and not speak a word when you're spoken to. I never saw such a boy! I'm going down stairs, this very minute, to tell my mother you've been hurting her beautiful gold watch!"

"Stop!" cried the boy, suddenly finding his voice; "I reckon I can fix it! I was meaning to tell ma! I only wanted to see that little thing inside that ticks. I'll bet I'll fix it. I didn't go to hurt it, Grace!"

"O, yes, you feel like you could mend

watches, and fire guns, and be soldiers and generals," said Grace, shaking her ringlets; "but I'm going right down to tell ma!"

Horace's lips curled with scorn.

"That's right, Gracie; run and *tell!*"

"But, Horace, I ought to tell," said Grace, meekly; "it's my duty! Isn't there a little voice at your heart, and don't it say, you've done wicked?"

"There's a voice there," replied the boy, pertly; "but it don't say what you think it does. It says, 'If your pa finds out about the watch, won't you catch it?'"

To do Horace justice, he did mean to tell his mother. He had been taught to speak the truth, and the whole truth, cost what it might. He knew that his parents could forgive almost anything sooner than a falsehood, or a cowardly concealment. Words cannot tell how Mr. Clifford hated deceit.

"When a *lie* tempts you, Horace," said he, "scorn it, if it looks ever so white! Put your foot on it, and crush it like a snake!"

Horace ate dry toast again this morning, but no one seemed to notice it. If he had dared look up, he would have seen that his father and mother wore sorrowful faces.

After breakfast, Mr. Clifford called him into the library. In the first place, he took to pieces the mangled watch, and showed him how it had been injured.

"Have you any right to meddle with things which belong to other people, my son?"

Horace's chin snuggled down into the hollow place in his neck, and he made no reply.

"Answer me, Horace."

"No, sir."

"It will cost several dollars to pay for

repairing this watch: don't you think the little boy who did the mischief should give part of the money?"

Horace looked distressed; his face began to twist itself out of shape.

"This very boy has a good many pieces of silver which were given him to buy fire-crackers. So you see, if he is truly sorry for his fault, he knows the way to atone for it."

Horace's conscience told him, by a twinge, that it would be no more than just for him to pay what he could for mending the watch.

"Have you nothing to say to me, my child?"

For, instead of speaking, the boy was working his features into as many shapes as if they had been made of gutta percha. This was a bad habit of his, though, when he was doing it, he had no idea of "making up faces."

His father told him he would let him have the whole day to decide whether he ought to give up any of his money. A tear trembled in each of Horace's eyes, but, before they could fall, he caught them on his thumb and forefinger.

"Now," continued Mr. Clifford, "I have something to tell you. I decided last night to enter the army."

"O, pa," cried Horace, springing up, eagerly; "mayn't I go, too?"

"You, my little son?"

"Yes, pa," replied Horace, clinging to his father's knee. "Boys go to wait on the generals and things! I can wait on you. I can comb your hair, and bring your slippers. If I could be a waiter, I'd go a flyin'."

"Poor child," laughed Mr. Clifford, stroking Horace's head, "you're such a very little boy, only eight years old!"

"I'm going on nine. I'll be nine next New Year's Gift-day," stammered Horace, the bright flush dying out of his cheeks. "O, pa, I don't want you to go, if I can't go too!"

Mr. Clifford's lips trembled. He took the little boy on his knee, and told him how the country was in danger, and needed all its brave men.

"I should feel a great deal easier about leaving my dear little family," said he, "if Horace never disobeyed his mother; if he did not so often fall into mischief; if he was always sure to *remember*."

The boy's neck was twisted around till his father could only see the back of his head.

"Look here, pa," said he, at last, throwing out the words one at a time, as if every
one weighed a whole pound; "I'll give ma
that money; I'll do it to-day."

"That's right, my boy! that's honest!
You have given me pleasure. Remember,
when you injure the property of another,
you should always make amends for it as
well as you can. If you do not, you're
unjust and dishonest."

I will not repeat all that Mr. Clifford said
to his little son. Horace thought then he
should never forget his father's good advice,
nor his own promises. We shall see whether
he did or not.

He was a restless, often a very naughty
boy; but when you looked at his broad
forehead and truthful eyes, you felt that,
back of all his faults, there was nobleness
in his boyish soul. His father often said,

"He will either make something or nothing;" and his mother answered, "Yes, there never will be any half-way place for Horace."

Now that Mr. Clifford had really enlisted, everybody looked sad. Grace was often in tears, and said, —

"We can't any of us live, if pa goes to the war."

But when Horace could not help crying, he always said it was because he "had the earache;" and perhaps he thought it was.

Mrs. Clifford tried to be cheerful, for she was a patriotic woman; but she could not trust her voice to talk a great deal, or sing much to the baby.

As for Barbara Kinckle, she scrubbed the floors, and scoured the tins, harder than ever, looking all the while as if every one of her friends was dead and buried. The family were to break up housekeeping, and Barbara was very sorry. Now she would have to go to her home, a little way back in the country, and work in the fields, as many German girls do every summer.

"O, my heart is sore," said she, "every time I thinks of it. They will in the cars go off, and whenever again I'll see the kliny (little) childers I knows not."

It was a sad day when Mr. Clifford bade good by to his family. His last words to Horace were these: "Always obey your mother, my boy, and remember that God sees all you do."

He was now "Captain Clifford," and went away at the head of his company, looking like, what he really was, a brave and noble gentleman.

Grace wondered if he ever thought of the bright new buttons on his coat; and

Horace walked about among his school-fellows with quite an air, very proud of being the son of a man who either was now, or was going to be, the greatest officer in Indiana!

If any body else had shown as much self-esteem as Horace did, the boys would have said he had "the *big* head." When Yankee children think a playmate conceited, they call him "stuck up;" but Hoosier children say he has "the *big* head." No one spoke in this way of Horace, however, for there was something about him which made every body like him, in spite of his faults.

He loved his play-fellows, and they loved him, and were sorry enough to have him go away; though, perhaps, they did not shed so many tears as Grace's little mates, who said, "they never'd have any more good times: they didn't mean to try."

Mrs. Clifford, too, left many warm friends, and it is safe to say, that on the morning the family started for the east, there were a great many people "crying their hearts out of their eyes." Still, I believe no one sorrowed more sincerely than faithful Barbara Kinckle.

CHAPTER III.

TAKING A JOURNEY.

It was a great effort for Mrs. Clifford to take a journey to Maine with three children; but she needed the bracing air of New England, and so did Grace and the baby.

To be sure they had the company of a gentleman who was going to Boston; but he was a very young man indeed, who thought a great deal more of his new mustache than he did of trunks, and checks, and tickets.

Twenty times a day Mrs. Clifford wished her husband could have gone with her before he enlisted, for she hardly knew what

to do with restless little Horace. As for
sitting still, it was more than the boy could
do. He would keep jerking his inquisitive
little head out of the window, for he never
remembered a caution five minutes. He
delighted to run up and down the narrow
aisle, and, putting his hands on the arms
of the seats, swing backward and forward
with all his might. He became acquainted
with every lozenge-boy and every newspaper-
boy on the route, and seemed to be in a
high state of merriment from morning till
night.

Grace, who was always proper and well-
behaved, was not a little mortified by Horace's rough manners.

" He means no harm," Mrs. Clifford would
say, with a smile and a sigh; " but, Mr. Lazelle, if you will be so kind as to watch
him a little, I will be greatly obliged."

Mr. Lazelle would reply, "O, certainly, madam; be quite easy about the child; he is not out of my sight for a moment!"

So saying, perhaps he would go in search of him, and find him under a seat playing with Pincher, his clothes covered with dust, and his cap lying between somebody's feet.

At such times Mr. Lazelle always said, — "Upon my word, you're a pretty little fellow!" and looked as if he would like to shake him, if it were not for soiling his gloves.

Horace laughed when Mr. Lazelle called him "a pretty little fellow," and thought it a fine joke. He laughed, too, when the young man told him to "come out," for there was something in the pettish tone of his voice which Horace considered very amusing.

"I'll wait till he gets through scolding,

and goes to coaxing," thought the boy : "he's a smart man! can't make such a little fellow mind! "

Mr. Lazelle was very much vexed with Horace, and firmly resolved that he would never again take charge of a lady travelling with children. At one time he flew into a passion, and boxed the boy's ears. Horace felt very much like a wounded wasp. He knew Mr. Lazelle would not have dared strike him before his mother, and from that moment he despised him as a " sneak."

Whenever Mr. Lazelle was looking for him in great haste, he was very likely to be missing; and when that sorely tried young gentleman was almost in despair, a saucy little head would appear at the car-window, and a small voice would shout, —

" Ho, Mr. Lazelle! why don't you come ahead? I beat you *in!* "

CAPTAIN HORACE LOST.   *Page 42.*

"Horace," said Mrs. Clifford, wearily, "you don't know how you tire me! Here is this dear baby that I have to hold in my arms; isn't it enough that I should have the care of him, without being all the while anxious about you?"

"Yes," chimed in Grace, pushing back her beautiful curls, "you don't know how ma and I fret about you. You'll kill poor ma before ever we can get you east!"

Horace hung his head for shame, and decided that it didn't "pay" to punish Mr. Lazelle, if his mother must suffer too. He meant, for her sake, to "turn over a new leaf," though he did not say so.

On the afternoon of their second day's ride, they reached the beautiful city of Cleveland. Here they were to rest for a few hours. Their clothes were sadly tumbled, their collars dust-color, and their faces and hair rough with cinders. A thorough washing and brushing, and some fresh ruffles and laces, gave a much tidier appearance to the whole party.

After Grace and Horace were ready, Mrs. Clifford thought they might as well go down stairs while she tried to rock little Katie to sleep.

"Be sure not to go away from the house," said she. "Grace, I depend upon you to take care of Horace, for he may forget."

The children had been standing on the piazza for some time, watching the people passing, while Mr. Lazelle lounged near by, talking politics with some gentlemen. In a little while Mrs. Clifford sent for Grace to go up stairs and amuse the poor baby, who could not be rocked to sleep.

For a few moments after she had gone

Horace stood near the door, still gazing into the street, when, suddenly, he heard a faint sound of martial music: a brass band was turning the corner. Soon they were in sight, men 'n handsome uniform, drawing music from various instruments, picking, blowing, or beating it out, as the case might be.

It was glorious, Horace thought. He could not keep still. He ran out, and threw up his cap before he knew it almost, shouting with delight, —

"Ho, Mr. Lazelle! ain't that jolly? Ho, Mr. Lazelle! where *are* you, anyhow?"

Probably, if the boy had stopped to think, he might have remembered that Mr. Lazelle was in the parlor; but no, Horace was sure he must have crossed the street to look at the band.

"I'm going, too," said he to himself.

"Of course, where Mr. Lazelle goes, I can go, for he has the care of me!"

With that he dashed headlong into the crowd, looking here, there, and everywhere for Mr. Lazelle.

But, O, that music! Did a little boy's boots ever stand still when a drum was playing, "March, march away"? No doubt his father was keeping step to just such sounds, on his path to martial glory! The fife and bugle whistled with magical voices, and seemed to say, —

"Follow, follow, follow on!"

And Horace followed; sometimes thinking he was in search of Mr. Lazelle, sometimes forgetting it altogether. He knew he was doing very wrong, but it seemed as if the music almost drowned the voice of his conscience.

In this way they turned street after street,

till, suddenly, the band and the crowd entered a large public building. Then the music died out, and with it the fire of eagerness in the little boy's soul.

Where *was* Mr. Lazelle? If he could see him now, he would forgive the boxed ears. How could he ever find his way back to the hotel? It had not as yet entered his head to ask any one.

He darted off at great speed, but, as it happened, in precisely the wrong direction. The houses grew smaller and farther apart, and presently he came to a high, sandy cliff overlooking the lake. Now the shades of night began to fall, and his stout heart almost failed him. The longing grew so strong to see mother, and Grace, and baby, that the tears would start, in spite of himself.

At last, just as he was wondering which

way to turn next, somebody touched his shoulder, and a rough voice said, —

"Hullo, my little man! What you doin' in this ward? Come; don't you pull away from me: I'm a city officer. Got lost, hey?"

Horace shook with fright. O dear, was it a crime, then, to get lost? He remembered all the stories he had ever heard of lock-ups, and state-prisons, and handcuffs.

"O, I didn't mean any harm, sir," cried he, trying to steady his voice; "I reckon I ain't lost, sir; or, if I am, I ain't lost *much!*"

"So, so," laughed the policeman, good-naturedly; "and what was your name, my little man, before you got lost, and didn't get lost *much?*"

"My name is Horace Clifford, sir," replied the boy, wondering why a cruel policeman should want to laugh.

"Well, well," said the man, not unkindly, "I'm glad I've come across ye, for your mother's in a terrible taking. What set ye out to run off? Come, now; don't be sulky. Give us your hand, and I guess, seein' it's you, we won't put you in the lock-up this time."

Horace was very grateful to the officer for not handcuffing him on the spot; still he felt as if it was a great disgrace to be marched through the city by a policeman.

Mrs. Clifford, Grace, and Mr. Lazelle met them on the way.

"O, my dear, dear son," cried Mrs. Clifford, as soon as she could speak; "do you know how you've frightened us all?"

"I followed the band," stammered Horace. 'I was looking for Mr. Lazelle."

"You're a naughty, mean little boy," cried Grace, when she had made sure he was not hurt anywhere. "It would have been good enough for you if you'd drowned in the lake, and the bears had ate you up!"

Still she kissed her naughty brother, and it was to be noticed that her eyelids were very red from crying.

"I'll never let go your hand again, Horace," said she, "till we get to grandma's. You're just as *slippery!*"

Mr. Lazelle looked as if it would be an immense relief to him if Miss Grace would keep her word; he thought he was undergoing a great trial with Horace.

"It's a shame," said he to himself, "that a perfect lady, like Mrs. Clifford, should have such a son! I'd enjoy whipping him — for her sake! Why in the world don't she *train* him?"

Mr. Lazelle did not know of the faithful talk Mrs Clifford had with Horace that night, nor how the boy's heart swelled with grief, and love, and new resolutions.

This adventure caused a day's delay, for it made the party too late for the boat. Horace was so sorry for his foolish conduct, that he spent the next day in the most subdued manner, and walked about the chamber on tiptoe, while Grace tried to soothe little Katie.

But, in crossing the lake, he "forgot" again. His mother allowed him to go up on the hurricane deck with Mr. Lazelle, just for ten minutes; and there he became acquainted with the pilot, who was struck with his intelligence, and freely answered all the questions he asked about the engine, "the whistle," and the steering.

"O, pshaw!" said Horace; "I'll make a steamboat myself, and give it to Grace for a present!"

Full of this new plan, he left the pilot
without so much as a "thank you," running
lown the steps, two at a time, unobserved
by Mr. Lazelle, who was playing the flute.
He wanted to see how the "rigging" was
made, and stopped to ask leave of nobody.

Down another flight of stairs, out across
trunks, and bales, and ropes, he pushed his
way to get a good sight of the deck. He
paid no heed to people or things, and nearly
ran over an Irish boy, who was drawing
up water in buckets for washing. Somebody shouted, "He's trying to kill hisself,
I do believe!"

Somebody rushed forward to seize the
daring child by the collar of his jacket, but
too late; he had fallen headlong into the
lake!

A scream went up from the deck that

pierced the air, — "Boy overboard! Help! help! help!"

Mrs. Clifford heard, and knew, by instinct, that it was Horace. She had just sent Grace to call him, not feeling safe to trust him longer with Mr. Lazelle. She rushed through the door of the state-room, and followed the crowd to the other side of the boat, crying, —

"O, can't somebody save him!"

There was no mistaking the mother's voice; the crowd made way for her.

"Safe! safe and sound!" was the shout now. "All right!"

The Irish lad, at Horace's first plunge, had thrown him his bucket — it was a life-preserver; that is, it would not sink — and the drowning boy had been drawn up by means of a rope attached to the bail.

"Ma," said Grace, when they were all

safely in the cars at Buffalo, and Horace as well as ever, though a little pale, "I do believe there never was anybody had such an awful journey! *Do* you suppose we'll ever get Horace home to grandma's?"

CHAPTER IV.

AT GRANDPA PARLIN'S.

It was over at last — the long, tedious journey, which Horace spoiled for everybody, and which nobody but Horace enjoyed.

When they drove up to the quiet old homestead at Willowbrook, and somebody had taken the little baby, poor Mrs. Clifford threw herself into her mother's arms, and sobbed like a child. Everybody else cried, too; and good, deaf grandpa Parlin, with smiles and tears at the same time, declared, —

"I don't know what the matter is; so I can't tell whether to laugh or cry."

Then his daughter Margaret went up and said in his best ear that they were just crying for joy, and asked him if that wasn't a silly thing to do.

Grace embraced everybody twice over; but Horace was a little shy, and would only give what his aunties called "canary kisses."

"Margaret, I want you to give me that darling baby this minute," said Mrs. Parlin, wiping her eyes. "Now you can bring the butter out of the cellar: it's all there is to be done, except to set the tea on the table."

Then grandma Parlin had another cry over little Katie: not such a strange thing, for she could not help thinking of Harry, the baby with sad eyes and pale face, who had been sick there all the summer before, and was now an angel. As little Prudy had said, "God took him up to heaven, but the tired part of him is in the garden."

Yes, under a weeping-willow. Every-body was thinking just now of tired little Harry, "the sweetest flower that ever was planted in that garden."

"Why, Maria," said Mrs. Clifford, as soon as she could speak, "how did you ever travel so far with this little, little baby?"

"I don't know, mother," replied Mrs. Clifford; "I think 1 could never have got here without Grace: she has been my little waiter, and Katie's little nurse."

Grace blushed with delight at this well-deserved praise.

"And Horace is so large now, that he was some help, too, I've no doubt," said his grandmother.

"I would have took the baby," cried Horace, speaking up very quickly, before any one else had time to answer, — "I would have took the baby, but she wouldn't let me."

Mrs. Clifford might have said that Horace himself had been as much trouble as the baby; but she was too kind to wound her little boy's feelings.

It was certainly a very happy party who met around the tea-table at Mr. Parlin's that evening. It was already dusk, and the large globe lamp, with its white porcelain shade, gave a cheery glow to the pleasant dining-room.

First, there was cream-toast, made of the whitest bread, and the sweetest cream.

"This makes me think of Mrs. Gray," said Mrs. Clifford, smiling; "I hope she is living yet."

"She is," said Margaret, "but twelve years old."

Grace looked up in surprise.

"Why, that's only a little girl, aunt Madge!"

"My dear, it's only a cow!"

"O, now I remember; the little blue one, with brass knobs on her horns!"

"Let's see; do you remember Dr. Quack and his wife?"

"O, yes'm! they were white ducks; and how they did swim! It was a year ago. I suppose Horace doesn't remember."

"Poh! yes, I do; they were *spin-footed!*"

"Why, Horace," said Grace, laughing; "you mean *web-footed!*"

Horace bent his eyes on his plate, and did not look up again for some time.

There was chicken-salad on the table. Margaret made that—putting in new butter, because she knew Mrs. Clifford did not like oil.

There was delicious looking cake, "some that had been touched with frost, and some that hadn't," as grandpa said, when he passed the basket.

But the crowning glory of the supper was a dish of scarlet strawberries, which looked as if they had been drinking dew-drops and sunshine till they had caught all the richness and sweetness of summer.

"O, ma!" whispered Grace, "I'm beginning to feel so happy! I only wish my father was here."

After tea, grandpa took Horace and Grace on each knee, large as they were, and sang some delightful evening hymns with what was left of his once fine voice. He looked so peaceful and happy, that his daughters were reminded of the Bible verse, "Children's children are the crown of old men."

"I think now," said Mrs. Clifford, coming back from putting the baby to sleep, "it's high time my boy and girl were saying, 'Good-night, and pleasant dreams.' "

"Aunt Madge is going up stairs with us; aren't you, auntie?"

"Yes, Horace; your other auntie wouldn't do, I suppose," said Louise. "That makes me think of the way this same Horace used to treat me when he was two years old. '*Her* can't put me to bed,' he would say; 'her's too *little*.'"

"I remember," said Margaret, "how he dreaded cold water. When his mother called him to be washed, and said, 'Ma doesn't want a little dirty boy,' he would look up in her face, and say, 'Does mamma want 'ittle *cold* boy?'"

The happy children kissed everybody good-night, and followed their aunt Madge up stairs. Now, there was a certain small room, whose one window opened upon the piazza, and it was called "the green chamber." It contained a cunning little bedstead, a wee bureau, a dressing-table, and washing-stand, all pea-green. It was a room which seemed to have been made and furnished on purpose for a child, and it had been promised to Grace in every letter aunt Madge had written to her for a year.

Horace had thought but little about the room till to-night, when his aunt led Grace into it, and he followed. It seemed so fresh and sweet in "the green chamber," and on the dressing-table there was a vase of flowers.

Aunt Madge bade the children look out of the window at a bird's nest, which was snuggled into one corner of the piazza-roof, so high up that nobody could reach it without a very tall ladder.

"Now," said aunt Madge, "the very first thing Grace hears in the morning will probably be bird-music."

Grace clapped her hands.

"And where am *I* going to sleep?" said

Horace, who had been listening, and looking on in silence. His aunt had forgotten that he was sometimes jealous; but she could not help knowing it now, for a very disagreeable expression looked out at his eyes, and drew down the corners of his mouth.

"Why, Horace dear, we have to put you in one of the back chambers, just as we did when you were here before; but you know it's a nice clean room, with white curtains, and you can look out of the window at the garden."

"But it's over the kitchen!"

"There, Horace," said Grace, "I'd be ashamed! You don't act like a little gen. tleman! What would pa say?"

"Why couldn't I have the big front chamber?" said the little boy, shuffling his feet, and looking down at his shoes.

"Because," said aunt Madge, smiling, "that is for your mother and the baby."

"But if I could have this little cunning room, I'd go a flyin'. Grace ain't company any more than me."

Aunt Madge remembered Horace's hit-or-miss way of using things, and thought of the elephant that once walked into a china shop.

Grace laughed aloud.

"Why, Horace Clifford, you'd make the room look like everything; you know you would! O, auntie, you ought to see how he musses up my cabinet! I have to hide the key; I do *so!*"

Horace took the room which was given him, but he left his sister without his usual good-night kiss, and when he repeated his prayer, I am afraid he was thinking all the while about the green chamber.

The next morning the children had intended to go into the garden bright and early. Grace loved flowers, and when she was a mere baby, just able to toddle into the meadow, she would clip off the heads of buttercups and primroses, hugging and kissing them like friends.

Horace, too, had some fancy for flowers, especially flaring ones, like sunflowers and hollyhocks. Dandelions were nice when the stems would curl without bothering, and poppies were worth while for little girls, he thought, because, after they are gone to seed, you can make them into pretty good teapots.

He wanted to go out in the garden now for humming-birds, and to see if the dirt-colored toad was still living in his "nest," in one of the flower-beds.

But the first thing the children heard in the morning was the pattering of rain on the roof. No going out to-day. Grace was

too tired to care much.   Horace felt cross;
but remembering how many messages his
grandmother had sent to her "good little
grandson," and how often aunt Madge had
written about "dear little Horace, the nephew
she was so proud of," he felt ashamed to go
down stairs scowling.   If his good-morning
smile was so thin that you could see a frown
through it, still it was better than no smile
at all.

The breakfast was very nice, and Horace
would have enjoyed the hot griddle-cakes
and maple sirup, only his aunt Louise, a
handsome young lady of sixteen, watched
him more than he thought was quite polite,
saying every now and then, —

"Isn't he the image of his father?   Just
such a nose, just such a mouth!   He eats
fast, too; that is characteristic!"

Horace did not know what "characteristic " meant, but thought it must be something bad, for with a child's quick eye he could see that his pretty aunt was inclined to laugh at him. In fact, he had quite an odd way of talking, and his whole appearance was amusing to Miss Louise, who was a very lively young lady.

"Horace, you were telling me last night about Mr. Lazelle: what did you say was the color of his coat?"

"I said it was *blueberry* color," replied Horace, who could see, almost without looking up, that aunt Louise was smiling at aunt Madge.

"He is a *musicianer* too, I think you said, and his hair *crimps*. Dear me, what a funny man!"

Horace was silent, and made up his mind that he should be careful another time what he said before aunt Louise.

Soon after breakfast he and Pincher went "up-attic" to see what they could find, while Grace followed her grandmother and aunties from parlor to kitchen, and from kitchen to pantry. She looked pale and tired, but was so happy that she sang every now and then at the top of her voice, forgetting that little Katie was having a nap.

Pretty soon Horace came down stairs with an old, rusty gun much taller than himself. Mrs. Clifford was shocked at first, but smiled the next moment, as she remembered what an innocent thing it was, past its "prime" before she was of Horace's age.

The little boy playfully pointed the gun towards Grace, who screamed with fright, and ran away as fast as she could.

"I don't care," cried she, coming back, a little ashamed at being laughed at · "how did *I* know it wasn't loaded? Do you think 'twould look well for a little girl *not* to be afraid of a gun?"

This speech amused everybody, particularly Horace, who was glad to have Grace say a foolish thing once in a while. It raised his self-esteem somehow; and, more than that, he liked to remember her little slips of the tongue, and tease her about them.

It was not long before he had seen all there was to be seen in the house, and wanted to "*do* something." As for reading, that was usually too stupid for Horace. Grace kindly offered to play checkers with him; but she understood the game so much better than he did, that she won at every trial.

This was more than he could bear with patience; and, whenever he saw that she was gaining upon him, he wanted to "turn it into a *nire-name*."

"But that isn't fair, Horace."

"Well, ma, just you see how mean Grace is! There, she wants me to jump that man yonder, so she'll take two of mine, and go right in the king-row!"

"But, Horace," said Grace, gently, "what do I play for if I don't try to beat?"

"There now," cried he, "chase my men up to the king-row, so I can't crown 'em, do!"

"Just what I'm doing," replied Grace, coolly.

"Well, I should think you'd better take 'em all, and be done with it! Before I'd be so mean as to set *traps!*"

"Look. Horace," said Grace; "you didn't jump when you ought to, and I'm going to *huff* your man. See, I blow it, just this way; old Mr. Knight calls it *huffing.*"

"Huff away then! but you stole one of those kings. I'll bet you stole it off the board after I jumped it."

"Now, Horace Clifford," cried Grace, with tears in her eyes, "I never did such a thing as to steal a king; and if you say so I won't play!"

"Horace," said Mrs. Clifford, who had been trying for some time to speak, "what do you play checkers for?"

"Ma'am? Why, to beat, of course."

"Well, do you consider it work, or play?"

"Work, or play? Why, it's a game, ma; so it's play."

"But Grace was so obliging that she wished to amuse you, my son. *Does* it amuse you? Doesn't it make you cross? Do you know that you have spoken a great many sharp words to your kind sister?

"Shut the board right up, my child; and remember from this time never to play checkers, or any other game, when you feel

yourself growing fretful! As you sometimes say, 'It doesn't pay.'"

Horace closed the board, looking ashamed.

"That's sound advice for everybody," said
aunt Madge, stroking her little nephew's
hair. "If children always remembered it,
they would get along more pleasantly together — I know they would."

Grace had been looking ill all the morning, and her mother now saw symptoms of
a chill. With all her tender anxiety she
had not known how tired her little daughter
was. It was two or three weeks before the
child was rested; and whenever she had a
chill, which was every third day for a while,
she was delirious, and kept crying out, —

"O, do see to Horace, mamma! Mr. Lazelle will forget! O, Horace, now *don't* let
go my hand! I've got the bundles, mamma,
and the milk for the baby."

And sometimes Mrs. Clifford would call Horace to come and take his sister's hand, just to assure her that he was not lying cold and dead in the waters of Lake Erie. It was really touching to see how heavily the cares of the journey had weighed on the dear girl's youthful spirits.

CHAPTER V.

CAPTAIN OF A COMPANY.

At first Mrs. Clifford thought she did not care about having the children go to school, as they had been kept at their studies for nearly nine months without a vacation, except Christmas holidays.

But what was to be done with Horace? Aunt Louise, who was not passionately fond of children, declared her trials were greater than she could bear. Grace was a little lady, she thought; but as for Horace, and his dog Pincher, and the "calico kitty," which he had picked up for a pet!—Louise disliked dogs and despised kittens. Sometimes, as she told Margaret, she felt as if she should certainly fly; sometimes she was sure she was going crazy; and then again it seemed as if her head would burst into a thousand pieces.

None of these dreadful accidents happened, it is true; but a great many other things did. Hammers, nails, and augers were carried off, and left to rust in the dew. A cup of green paint, which for months had stood quietly on an old shelf in the storeroom, was now taken down and stirred with a stick, and all the toys which Horace whittled out were stained green, and set in the sun to dry. A pair of cheese-tongs, which hung in the back room, a boot-jack, the washing-bench, which was once red, — all became green in a very short time : only the red of the bench had a curious effect, peeping out from its light and ragged coat of green.

The blue sled which belonged to Susy and Prudy, was brought down from the shed-chamber, and looked at for some time. It would present a lovely appearance, Horace thought, if he only dared cross it off with green. But as the sled belonged to his little cousins, and they were not there to see for themselves how beautiful he could make it look, why, he must wait till they came; and then, very likely, the paint would be gone.

Of course, Horace soiled his clothes sadly : "that was always just like him," his aunt Louise said.

This was not all. A little neighbor, Gilbert Brown, came to the house at all hours, and between the two boys there was a noise of driving nails, firing pop-guns, shouting and running from morning till night.

They built a "shanty" of the boards which grandpa was saving to mend the fence, and in this shanty they "kept store," trading in crooked pins, home-made toys, twine, and jack-knives.

"Master chaps, them children are," said Abner, the good-natured hired man.

"Hard-working boys! They are as destructive as army-worms," declared grandpa, frowning, with a twinkle in his eye.

Horace had a cannon about a foot long, which went on wheels, with a box behind it, and a rammer lashed on at the side — not to mention an American flag which floated over the whole. With a stout string he drew his cannon up to the large oilnut tree, and then with a real bayonet fixed to a wooden gun, he would lie at full length under the shade, calling himself a sharpshooter guarding the cannon. At these times woe to the "calico kitty," or Grace, or anybody else who happened to go near him! for he gave the order to "charge," and the charge was made most vigorously.

Upon the whole, it was decided that everybody would feel easier and happier if Horace should go to school. This plan did not please him at all, and he went with sulky looks and a very bad grace.

His mother sighed; for though her little boy kept the letter of the law, which says, "Children, obey your parents," he did not do it in the *spirit* of the commandment, "*Honor* thy father and thy mother."

In a thousand ways Mrs. Clifford was made unhappy by Horace, who should have been a comfort to her. It was sad, indeed; for never did a kind mother try harder to "train up a child" in the right way.

It did not take Horace a great while to

renew his acquaintance with the schoolboys, who all seemed to look upon him as a sort of curiosity.

"I never knew before," laughed little Dan Rideout, "that my name was Dan-yell!"

"He calls a pail a bucket, and a dipper a *tin-kup*," said Gilbert Brown.

"Yes," chimed in Willy Snow, "and he asks, 'Is school *took up?*' just as if it was knitting-work that was on needles."

"How he rolls his r's!" said Peter Grant. "You can't say hor-r-se the way he does! I'll bet *the ain't* a boy can do it, unless it's a Cahoojack." Peter meant *Hoosier*.

"Well, I wouldn't be seen saying *hoss*," returned Horace, with some spirit; "that's *Yankee*."

"I guess the Yankees are as good as the Cahoojacks: wasn't your mother a Yankee?"

"Yes," faltered Horace; "she was born up

north here, in the Frigid Zone ; but she isn't so much relation to me as my father is, for her name wasn't Clifford. She wouldn't have been *any* relation to me if she hadn't married my father ! "

One or two of the larger boys laughed at this speech, and Horace, who could never endure ridicule, stole quietly away.

"Now, boys, you behave," said Edward Snow, Willy's older brother; "he's a smart little fellow, and it's mean to go to hurting his feelings. Come back here, Spunky Clifford; let's have a game of *hi spy!*"

Horace was "as silent as a stone."

"He don't like to be called Spunky Clifford," said Johnny Bell; "do you, Horace?"

"The reason I don't like it," replied the boy, "is because it's not my name."

"Well, then," said Edward Snow, winking

to the other boys, "won't you play with us, *Master Horace?*"

"I'll not go back to be laughed at," replied he, stoutly : "when I'm home I play with Hoosier boys, and they're politer than Yankees."

"'Twas only those big boys," said Johnny Bell; "now they've gone off. Come, let's play something."

"I should think you'd be willing for us to laugh," added honest little Willy Snow; "we can't help it, you talk so funny. We don't mean anything."

"Well," said Horace, quite restored to good humor, and speaking with some dignity, "you may laugh at me *one* kind of a way, but if you mean *humph* when you laugh, I won't stand it."

"*Woon't* stand it!" echoed Peter Grant; "ain't that Dutch?"

"Dutch?" replied Horace : "I'll show you what *Dyche* is! We have a *Dyche* teacher come in our school every day, and he stamps his foot and tears round! 'Sei ruhig,' he says : that means, 'hush your mouth and keep still.' "

"Is he a Jew, and does he stay in a synagogue?"

"No, he is a German *Luteran*, or a Dutch *Deformed*, or something that way."

"What do you learn in?" said Johnny Bell.

"Why, in little German Readers : what else would they be?"

"Does it read like stories and verses?"

'I don't know. He keeps hitting the books with a little switch, and screamin' out as if the house was afire."

"Come, say over some Dutch; *woon't* you, Horace?"

So the little boy repeated some German poetry, while his schoolmates looked up at him in wonder and admiration. This was just what Horace enjoyed; and he continued, with sparkling eyes, —

"I s'pose you can't any of you *count* Dutch?"

The boys confessed that they could not.

"It's just as easy," said Horace, telling over the numbers up to twenty, as fast as he could speak.

"You can't any of you *write* Dutch; can you? You give me a slate now, and I'll write it all over so you couldn't read a word of it."

"Ain't it very hard to make?" asked the boys in tones of respectful astonishment.

"I reckon you'd think 'twas hard, it's so full of little quirls, but *I* can write it as easy as English."

This was quite true, for Horace made very hard work of any kind of writing.

It was not two days before he was at the head of that part of the school known as "the small boys," both in study and play; yet everybody liked him, for, as I have said before, the little fellow had such a strong sense of justice, and such kindness of heart, that he was always a favorite, in spite of his faults.

The boys all said there was nothing "mean" about Horace. He would neither abuse a smaller child, nor see one abused. If he thought a boy was doing wrong, he was not afraid to tell him so, and you may be sure he was all the more respected for his moral courage.

Horace talked to his schoolmates a great deal about his father, Captain Clifford, who was going to be a general some day.

"When I was home," said he, "I studied pa's book of *tictacs*, and I used to drill the boys."

There was a loud cry of "Why can't you drill us? Come, let's us have a company, and you be cap'n!"

Horace gladly consented, and the next Saturday afternoon a meeting was appointed at the "Glen." When the time came, the boys were all as joyful as so many squirrels suddenly let out of a cage.

"Now look here, boys," said Horace, brushing back his "shingled hair," and walking about the grove with the air of a lord. "First place, if I'm going to be captain, you must mind; will you? *say*."

Horace was not much of a public speaker; he threw words together just as it happened; but there was so much meaning in the twistings of his face, the jerkings of his head, and the twirlings of his thumbs, that if you were looking at him you must know what he meant.

"Ay, ay!" piped the little boys in chorus.

"Then I'll muster you in," said Horace, grandly. "Has everybody brought their guns?—I mean *sticks*, you know!"

"Ay, ay!"

"I want to be corporal," said Peter Grant.

"I'll be major," cried Willy Snow.

"There, you've spoke," shouted the captain. "I wish there was a tub or bar'l to stand you on when you talk."

After some time an empty flour barrel was brought, and placed upright under a tree, to serve as a dunce-block.

"Now we'll begin 'new," said the captain. "Those that want to be mustered, rise up their hands; but don't you snap your fingers."

The caution came too late for some of the boys; but Horace forgave the seeming disrespect, knowing that no harm was intended

"Now, boys, what are you fighting about? — Say, For our country!"

"For our country," shouted the soldiers, some in chorus, and some in solo.

"And our flag," added Horace, as an after-thought.

"And our flag," repeated the boys, looking at the little banner of stars and stripes, which was fastened to the stump of a tree, and faintly fluttered in the breeze.

"Long may it wave!" cried Horace, growing enthusiastic, and pointing backward to the flag with a sweep of his thumb.

"There ain't a 'Secesh' in this company; there ain't a man but wants our battle to beat! If there is, we'll muster him out double-quick."

A few caps were flourished in the air, and every mouth was set firmly together, as if it would shout scorn of secession if it dared speak. It was a loyal company; there was no doubt of that. Indeed, the captain was so bitter against the South, that he had asked his aunt Madge if it was right to let *south-ernwood* grow in the garden.

"Now," said Horace, "Forward! March! 'Ploy column!—No, form a line first. Ten-*tion!*"

A curved, uncertain line, not unlike the letter S, gradually straightened itself, and the boys looked down to their feet as if they expected to see a chalk-mark on the grass.

"Now, when I say, 'Right!' you must look at the buttons on my jacket — or on yours, I've forgot which; on yours, I reckon. Right! Right at 'em! Right at the buttons!"

Obedient to orders, every boy's head drooped in a moment.

"Stop!" said Horace, knitting his brows; "that's enough!" For there seemed to be something wrong, he could not tell what.

"Now you may ''bout face;' that means whirl round. Now march! one, two, quick time, double-quick!"

"They're stepping on my toes," cried barefooted Peter Grant.

"Hush right up, private, or I'll stand you on the bar'l."

"I wish't you would," groaned little Peter; "it hurts."

"Well, then, I shan't," said the captain, decidedly, "for 'twouldn't be any punishin'. —Can't some of you whistle?"

Willy Snow struck up Yankee Doodle, which soon charmed the wayward feet of the little volunteers, and set them to march‧ing in good time.

Afterward their captain gave instructions in "groundin' arms," 'stackin' arms," "firin'," and "countin' a march," by which he meant "countermarching." He had really read a good many pages in Infantry Tactics, and had treasured up the military phrases with some care, though he had but a confused idea of their meaning.

"Holler-square!" said he, when he could think of nothing else to say. Of course he meant a "hollow square."

"Shall we holler all together?" cried a voice from the midst of the ranks.

The owner of the voice would have been "stood on the barrel," if Horace had been less busy thinking.

"I've forgot how they holler, as true as you live; but I reckon it's all together, and open your mouths wide."

At this the young volunteers, nothing

STAND BY THE FLAG. — Page 85.

loath, gave a long, deafening shout, which the woods caught up and echoed

Horace scratched his head. He had seen his father drill his men, but he could not remember that he had ever heard them scream.

A pitched battle came off next, which would have been a very peaceful one if all the boys had not wanted to be Northerners. But the feeling was greatly changed when Horace joined the Southern ranks, saying "he didn't care how much he played Secesh when everybody knew he was a good Union man, and his father was going to be a general." After this there was no trouble about raising volunteers on the rebel side.

The whole affair ended very pleasantly, only there was some slashing right and left with a few bits of broken glass, which were used as swords; and several mothers had wounds to dress that night.

Mrs. Clifford heard no complaint from her little son, although his fingers were quite ragged, and must have been painful. Horace was really a brave boy, and always bore suffering like a hero. More than that, he had the satisfaction of using the drops of blood for red paint; and the first thing after supper he made a wooden sword and gun, and dashed them **with red streaks**.

CHAPTER VI.

SUSY AND PRUDY.

THE Clifford children were very anxious to see Susy and Prudy, and it seemed a long while to wait; but the Portland schools had a vacation at last, and then it was time to expect the little cousins.

The whole family were impatient to see them and their excellent mother. Grandma lost her spectacles very often that afternoon, and every time she went to the window to look out, the ball of her knitting-work followed her, as Grace said, "like a little kitten."

There was great joy when the stage really

drove up to the door. The cousins were
rather shy of each other at first, and Prudy
hid her face, all glowing with smiles and
blushes, in her plump little hands. But the
stiffness wore away, and they were all as
well acquainted as ever they had been, in
about ten minutes.

"Ain't that a bumpin' stage, though?"
cried Horace; "just like a baby-jumper."

"We came in it, you know, Susy," said
Grace; "didn't it shake like a corn-popper?"

"I want to go and see the piggy and
ducks," said Prudy.

"Well," whispered Susy, "wait till after
supper."

The Cliffords were delighted with their
little cousins. When they had last seen
Prudy, which was the summer before, they
had loved her dearly. Now she was past
five, and "a good deal cunninger than ever;"

or so Horace thought. He liked her pretty face, her gentle ways, and said very often, f he had such a little sister he'd "go a lyin'."

To be sure Susy was just his age, and could run almost as fast as he could; still Horace did not fancy her half as much as Prudy, who could not run much without falling down, and who was always sure to cry if she got hurt.

Grace and Susy were glad that Horace liked Prudy so well, for when they were cutting out dolls' dresses, or playing with company, it was pleasant to have him take her out of the way.

Prudy's mouth was not much larger than a button-hole, but she opened it as wide as she could when she saw Horace whittle out such wonderful toys.

He tried to be as much as possible like a

man; so he worked with his jacket off, whistling all the while; and when he pounded, he drew in his breath with a whizzing noise, such as he had heard carpenters make.

All this was very droll to little Prudy, who had no brothers, and supposed her "captain cousin" must be a very remarkable boy, especially as he told her that, if he hadn't left his tool-box out west, he could have done "a heap better." It was quite funny to see her standing over him with such a happy, wondering little face, sometimes singing snatches of little songs, which were sure to be wrong somewhere, such as, —

> "Little kinds of *deedness*,
> Little words of love,
> Make this *earthen needn't*,
> Like the heaven above."

She thought, as Horace did, that her sled

would look very well "crossed off with green;" but Susy would not consent. So Horace made a doll's sled out of shingles, with turned-up runners, and a tongue of string. This toy pleased Prudy, and no one had a right to say it should not be painted green.

But as Captain Horace was just preparing to add this finishing touch, a lady arrived with little twin-boys, four years old. Aunt Madge came into the shed to call Horace and Prudy. "O, auntie," said Horace, "I don't believe I care to play with those little persons!"

His aunt smiled at hearing children called "little persons," but told Horace it would not be polite to neglect his young visitors: it would be positively rude. Horace did not wish to be considered an ill-mannered boy, and at last consented to have his hands and garments cleansed with turpentine to erase the paint, and to go into the nursery to see the "little persons."

It seemed to him and Prudy that the visit lasted a great while, and that it was exceedingly hard work to be polite.

When it was well over, Prudy said, "The next lady that comes here, I hope she won't bring any little *double boys!* What do I love little boys for, 'thout they're my cousins?"

After the sled was carefully dried, Horace printed on it the words "Lady Jane," in large yellow letters. His friend Gilbert found the paint for this, and it was thought by both the boys that the sled could not have been finer if "Lady Jane" had been spread on with gold-leaf by a sign-painter.

"Now, Prudy," said Horace, "it isn't everybody can make such a sled as that!

It's right strong, too; as strong as — why, it's strong enough to 'bear up an egg'!"

If Horace had done only such innocent things as to "drill" the little boys, make sleds for Prudy, and keep store with Gilbert, his mother might have felt happy.

But Horace was growing careless. His father's parting words, "Always obey your mother, my son, and remember that God sees all you do," did not often ring in his ears now. Mr. Clifford, though a kind parent, had always been strict in discipline, and his little son had stood in awe of him. Now that he had gone away, there seemed to be some danger that Horace might fall into bad ways. His mother had many serious fears about him, for, with her feeble health, and the care of little Katie, she could not be as watchful of him as she wished to be. She remembered how Mr. Clifford had often said, "He will either make something or nothing," and she had answered, "Yes, there'll never be any half-way place for Horace." She sighed now as she repeated her own words.

In his voyages of discovery Horace had found some gunpowder. "Mine!" said he to himself; "didn't aunt Madge say we could have everything we found up-attic?"

He knew that he was doing wrong when he tucked the powder slyly into his pocket. He knew he did wrong when he showed it to Gilbert, saying, —

"Got any matches, Grasshopper?"

They dug holes in the ground for the powder, and over the powder crossed some dry sticks. When they touched it off they ran away as fast as possible; but it was a wonder they were not both blown up. It was pleasant, no doubt, to hear the popping of the powder; but they dared not laugh too loud, lest some one in the house should hear them, and come out to ask what they could be playing that was so remarkably funny.

Mrs. Clifford little thought what a naughty thing Horace had been doing, when she called him in one day, and said, with a smiling face, — for she loved to make him happy, — "See, my son, what I have bought for you! It is a present from your father, for in his last letter he asked me to get it."

Horace fairly shouted with delight when he saw the beautiful Zouave suit, gray, bordered with red, and a cap to match. If he had any twinges of conscience about receiving this present, nobody knew it.

Here is the letter of thanks which he wrote to his father: —

7

"DEAR PAPA.

"I am sorry to say I have not seen you since you went to the war. Grandpa has two pigs. I want a drum so much!

"We have lots of squirrels: they chip. We have orioles: they say, 'Here, here, *here* I be!'

"I want the drum because I am a *captain!* We are going to train with paper caps.

"I get up the cows and have a good time.

"Good-by. From your son,

"HORACE P. CLIFFORD.

"P. S. Ma bought me the soldier clothes. I thank you."

About this time Mrs. Clifford was trying to put together a barrel of nice things to send to her husband. Grandma and aunt Madge baked a great many loaves of cake and hundreds of cookies, and put in cans of fruit and boxes of jelly wherever there was room. Aunt Louise made a nice little dressing-case of bronze kid, lined with silk, and Grace made a pretty pen-wiper and pin-ball. Horace whittled out a handsome steamboat, with *green* pipes, and the figure-head of an old man's face carved in wood. But Horace thought the face looked like Prudy's, and named the steamboat "The Prudy." He also broke open his savings-bank, and begged his mother to lay out all the money he had in presents for the sick soldiers.

"Horace has a kind and loving heart," said Margaret to Louise. "To be sure he won't keep still long enough to let anybody kiss him, but he really loves his parents dearly."

"Well, he's a terrible try-patience," said Louise.

"Wait a while! He is wilful and naughty,

but he never tells wrong stories. I think
there's hope of a boy who *scorns a lie!*
See if he doesn't come out right, Louise.
Why, I expect to be proud of our Horace
one of these days!"

CHAPTER VII.

IN THE WOODS.

"O. MA," said Horace, coming into the house one morning glowing with excitement, "mayn't I go in the woods with Peter Grant? He knows where there's heaps of boxberries."

" And who is Peter Grant, my son?"

"He is a little boy with a bad temper," said aunt Louise, frowning severely at Horace. — If she had had her way, I don't know but every little boy in town would have been tied to a bed-post by a clothes-line. As I have already said, aunt Louise was not remarkably fond of children, and when they were naughty it was hard for her to forgive them.

She disliked little Peter; but she never stopped to think that he had a cross and ignorant mother, who managed him so badly that he did not care about trying to be good. Mrs. Grant seldom talked with him about God and the Saviour; she never read to him from the Bible, nor told him to say his prayers.

Mrs. Clifford answered Horace that she did not wish him to go into the woods, and that was all that she thought it necessary to say.

Horace, at the time, had no idea of disobeying his mother; but not long afterwards he happened to go into the kitchen, where his grandmother was making beer.

"What do you make it of, grandma?" said he.

"Of molasses and warm water and yeast."

"But what gives the taste to it?"

"O, I put in spruce, or boxberry, or sarsaparilla."

"But see here, grandma: wouldn't you like to have me go in the woods 'some-place,' and dig roots for you?"

"Yes, indeed, my dear," said she inno-cently; "and if you should go, pray get some wintergreen, by all means."

Horace's heart gave a wicked throb of delight. If some one wanted him to go *after* something, of course he *ought* to go; for his mother had often told him he must try to be useful. Strolling into the woods with Peter Grant, just for fun, was very different from going in soberly to dig up roots for grandma.

He thought of it all the way out to the gate. To be sure he might go and ask his

mother again, but "what was the use, when
he knew certain sure she'd be willing?
Besides, wasn't the baby crying, so he
mustn't go in the room?"

These reasons sounded very well; but
they could be picked in pieces, and Horace
knew it. It was only when the baby was
asleep that he must keep out of the chamber; and, as for being sure that his mother
would let him go into the woods, the truth
was, he dared not ask her, for he knew she
would say, "No."

He found Peter Grant lounging near the
school-house, scribbling his name on the
clean white paint under one of the windows.

Peter's black eyes twinkled.

"Going, ain't you, cap'n! dog and all?
But where's your basket? Wait, and I'll
fetch one."

"There," said he, coming back again, "I

got that out of the stable there at the tavern; Billy Green is hostler: Billy knows me."

"Well, Peter, come ahead."

"I don't believe you know your way in these ere woods," returned Peter, with an air of importance. "I'll go fust. It's a mighty long stretch, 'most up to Canada; but I could find *my* way in the dark. I never got lost anywheres yet!"

"Poh! nor I either," Horace was about to say; but remembering his adventure in Cleveland, he drowned the words in a long whistle.

They kept on up the steep hill for some distance, and then struck off into the forest. The straight pine trees stood up solemn and still. Instead of tender leaves, they bristled all over with dark green "needles." They had no blessings of birds' nests in their branches ; yet they gave out a pleasant odor, which the boys said was "nice."

"But they aren't so splendid, Peter, as our trees out west — don't begin! *They* grow so big you can't chop 'em down. I'll leave it to Pincher!"

"Chop 'em down? I reckon it can't be done!" replied Pincher — not in words, but by a wag of his tail.

"Well, how *do* you get 'em down then, cap'n?"

"We cut a place right 'round 'em : that's girdlin' the tree, and then, ever so long after, it dies and drops down itself."

"O, my stars!" cried Peter, "I want to know!"

"No, you DON'T want to know, Peter, for I just told you! You may say, 'I wonder,' if you like : that's what we say out west."

"Wait," said Peter. "I only said, 'I want

to know what other trees you have;' that's what I meant, but you *shet* me right up."

"O, there's the butternut, and tree of heaven, and papaw, and 'simmon, and a 'right smart sprinkle' of wood-trees."

" What's a 'simmon?"

"O, it looks like a little baked apple, all wrinkled up; but it's right sweet. Ugh!" added Horace, making a wry face; "you better look out when they're green: they pucker your mouth up a good deal worse'n choke-cherries."

"What's a papaw?"

"A papaw? Well, it's a curious thing, not much account. The pigs eat it. It tastes like a custard, right soft and mellow. Come, let's go to work."

"Well, what's a tree of heaven?"

"O, Peter, for pity's sakes how do I know? It's a tree of heaven, I suppose.

It has pink hollyhocks growing on it. What makes you ask so many questions?"

Upon that the boys went to work picking boxberry leaves, which grew at the roots of the pine trees, among the soft moss and last year's cones. Horace was very anxious to gather enough for some beer; but it was strange how many it took to fill such "*enormous* big baskets."

"Now," said Horace, "I move we look over yonder for some wintergreen. You said you knew it by sight."

"Wintergreen? wintergreen?" echoed Peter: "O, yes, I know it well enough. It spangles 'round. See, here's some; the girls make wreaths of it."

It was *moneywort*; but Horace never doubted that Peter was telling the truth, and supposed his grandmother would be delighted to see such quantities of wintergreen.

After some time spent in gathering this, Horace happened to remember that he wanted sarsaparilla.

"I reckon," thought he, "they'll be glad I came, if I carry home so many things."

Peter knew they could find sarsaparilla, for there was not a root of any sort which did not grow "in the pines;" of that he was sure. So they struck still deeper into the woods, every step taking them farther from home. Pincher followed, as happy as a dog can be; but, alas! never dreaming that serious trouble was coming.

The boys dug up various roots with their jackknives; but they both knew the taste of sarsaparilla, and could not be deceived.

"We hain't come to it yet," said Peter; "but it's round here somewheres, I'll bet a dollar."

"I'm getting hungry," said Horace: "isn't it about time for the dinner-bell to ring?"

"Pretty near," replied Peter, squinting his eyes and looking at the sky as if there was a noon-mark up there, and he was the boy to find it. "That bell will ring in fifteen minutes: you see if it don't."

But it did not, though it was high noon, certainly. Hours passed. Horace remembered they were to have had salt codfish and cream gravy for dinner. Aunt Madge had said so; also a roly-poly with foaming sauce. It must now be long ago since the sugar and butter were beaten together for that sauce. He wondered if there would be any pudding left. He was sure he should like it cold, and a glass of water with ice in it.

O, how many times he could have gone to the barrel which stood by the sink, and drunk such deep draughts of water, when he didn't care anything about it! But now he was so thirsty, and there was not so much as a teaspoonful of water to be found!

"I motion we go home," said Horace, for at least the tenth time.

"Well," replied Peter, sulkily, "ain't we striking a bee-line?"

"We've got turned round," said Horace: "Canada is over yonder, *I* know."

"Pshaw! no, it ain't, no such a thing."

But they were really going the wrong way. The village bell had rung at noon, as usual, but they were too far off to hear it. It was weary work winding in and out, in and out, among the trees and stumps. With torn clothes, bleeding hands, and tired feet, the poor boys pushed on.

"Of course we're right," said Peter, in a would-be brave tone: "don't you remember that stump?"

"No, I don't, Peter Grant," replied Horace, who was losing his patience: "I never was here before. Humph! I thought you could find your way with your eyes shut."

"Turn and go t'other way, then," said Peter, adding a wicked word I cannot repeat.

"I will," replied Horace, coolly: "if I'd known you used such swearing words I never'd have come!"

"Hollo, there!" shouted Peter, a few moments after, "I'll keep with you, and risk it, cap'n."

"Come on, then," returned Horace, who was glad of Peter's company just now, little as he liked him. "Where's our baskets?" said he, stopping short.

"Sure enough," cried Peter; "but we can't go back now."

They had not gone far when they were startled by a cry from Pincher, a sharp cry of pain. He stood stock still, his brown eyes almost starting from their sockets with agony and fear. It proved that he had stumbled upon a fox-trap which was concealed under some dry twigs, and his right fore-paw was caught fast.

Here was a dilemma. The boys tried with all their might to set poor Pincher free; but it seemed as if they only made matters worse.

"What an old nuisance of a dog!" cried Peter; "just as we'd got to goin' on the right road."

"Be still, Peter Grant! Hush your mouth! If you say a word against my dog you'll catch it. Poor little Pincher!" said Horace, patting him gently and laying his cheek down close to his face.

The suffering creature licked his hands, and said with his eloquent eyes, —

8

"Dear little master, don't take it to heart! You didn't know I'd get hurt! You've always been good to poor Pincher."

"I'd rather have given a dollar," said Horace; "O, Pincher! I wish 'twas my foot; I tell you I do!"

They tried again, but the trap held the dog's paw like a vice.

"I'll tell you what," said Peter; "we'll leave the dog here, and go home and get somebody to come."

"You just behave, Peter Grant," said Horace, looking very angry. "I shouldn't want to be *your* dog! Just you hold his foot still, and I'll try again."

This time Horace examined the trap on all sides, and, being what is called an ingenious boy, did actually succeed at last in getting little Pincher's foot out.

"Whew! I didn't think you could," said Peter, admiringly.

"You couldn't, Peter; you haven't sense enough."

The foot was terribly mangled, and Pincher had to be carried home in arms.

"I should like to know, Peter, who set that trap. If my father was here, he'd have him in the lock-up."

"Poh! it wasn't set for dogs," replied Peter, in an equally cross tone, for both the boys were tired, hungry, and out of sorts. "Don't you know nothin'? That's a bear-trap!"

"A bear-trap! Do you have bears up here?"

"O, yes, dear me, suz: hain't you seen none since you've been in the State of Maine? I've ate 'em lots of times."

Peter had once eaten a piece of bear-steak, or it might have been moose-meat, he was not sure which; but at any rate it had been brought down from Moosehead Lake.

"Bears 'round here?" thought Horace, in a fright.

He quickened his pace. O, if he could only be sure it was the right road! Perhaps they were walking straight into a den of bears. He hugged little Pincher close in his arms, soothing him with pet names; for the poor dog continued to moan.

"O, dear, dear!" cried Peter, "don't you feel awfully?"

"I don't stop to think of my feelings," replied Horace, shortly.

"Well, I wish we hadn't come — I do."

"So do I, Peter. I won't play 'hookey' again; but I'm not a-goin' to cry."

"I'll never go anywheres with you any more as long as I live, Horace Clifford!"

"Nobody wants you to, Pete Grant!"

Then they pushed on in dignified silence, till Peter broke forth again with wailing sobs.

"I dread to get home! O, dear, I'll have to take it, I tell you. I guess you'd cry if you expected to be whipped."

Horace made no reply. He did not care about telling Peter that he too had a terrible dread of reaching home, for there was something a great deal worse than a whipping, and that was, a mother's sorrowful face.

"I shouldn't care if she'd whip me right hard," thought Horace; "but she'll talk to me about God and the Bible, and O, she'll look so white!"

"Peter, you go on ahead," said he aloud.

"What for?"

"O, I want to rest a minute with Pincher."

It was some moments before Peter would go, and then he went grumbling. As soon

as he was out of sight, Horace threw himself on his knees and prayed in low tones, —

"O God, I do want to be a good boy ; and
if I ever get out of this woods I'll begin!
Keep the bears off, please do, O God, and
let us find the way out, and forgive me.
Amen."

Horace had never uttered a more sincere
prayer in his life. Like many older people,
he waited till he was in sore need before he
called upon God; but when he had once
opened his heart to him, it was wonderful
how much lighter it felt.

He rose to his feet and struggled on, saying to Pincher, "Poor fellow, poor fellow,
don't cry: we'll soon be home."   .

"Hollo there, cap'n!" shouted Peter:
"we're comin' to a clearin'."

"Just as I expected," thought Horace:
"why didn't I pray to God before?"

IN THE WOODS. — Page 111.

CHAPTER VIII.

CAPTAIN CLIFFORD.

WHEN Horace entered the yard, holding the poor dog in his arms, he felt wretched indeed. At that moment all the sulkiness and self-will were crushed out of his little heart. It seemed to him that never, never had there lived upon the earth another boy so wicked as himself.

He forgot the excuses he had been making up about going into the woods because his grandmother wanted him to: he scorned to add falsehood to disobedience, and was more than willing to take his full share of blame.

"If ma would whip me like everything,
thought the boy, "I know I'd feel better."

It was a long, winding path from the gate.
The grounds looked very beautiful in the
golden light of the afternoon sun.   The
pink clover-patch nodded with a thousand
heads, and sprinkled the air with sweetness.

Everything was very quiet: no one was
on the piazza, no one at the windows.   The
blinds were all shut, and you could fancy
that the house had closed its many eyes and
dropped asleep.   There was an awe about
such perfect silence.   "Where could Grace
be, and those two dancing girls, Susy and
Prudy?"

He stole along to the back door, and
lifted the latch.   His grandmother stopped
with a bowl of gruel in her hand, and said,
"O, Horace!" that was all; but she could say
no more for tears.   She set down the bowl,

and went up to him, trying to speak; but the words trembled on her lips unspoken.

"O, grandma!" said Horace, setting little Pincher down on a chair, and clutching the skirt of her dress, "I've been right bad: I'm sorry — I tell you I am."

His grandmother had never heard him speak in such humble tones before.

"O, Horace!" she sobbed again, this time clasping him close to her heart, and kissing him with a yearning fondness she had hardly ever shown since he was a little toddling baby. "My darling, darling boy!"

Horace thought by her manner they must all have been sadly frightened about him.

"I got lost in the woods, grandma; but it didn't hurt me any, only Pincher got his foot caught."

"Lost in the woods?" repeated she: "Grace thought you went home to dinner with Willy Snow."

So it seemed they had not worried about him at all: then what was grandma crying about?

"Don't go up stairs, dear," said she, as he brushed past her and laid his hand on the latch of the chamber door.

"But I want to see ma."

"Wait a little," said Mrs. Parlin, with a fresh burst of tears.

"Why, what *is* the matter, grandma; and where's Grace, and Susy, and Prudy?"

"Grace is with your mother, and the other children are at aunt Martha's. But if you've been in the woods all day, Horace, you must be very hungry."

"You've forgot Pincher, grandma."

The boy would not taste food till the dog's foot had been bandaged, though, all the while his grandmother was doing up the wound, it seemed to Horace that she must be thinking of something else, or she would pity Pincher a great deal more.

The cold dinner which she set out on the table was very tempting, and he ate heartily; but after every mouthful he kept asking, "What could be the matter? Was baby worse? Had anybody took sick?"

But his grandmother stood by the stove stirring gruel, and would answer him nothing but, "I'll let you know very soon."

She wanted the little boy to be rested and refreshed by food before she told him a very painful thing. Then she took him up stairs with her into her own chamber, which was quite shady with grape-vines, and so still that you could only hear the buzzing of two or three flies.

She had brought a bowl of hot gruel on a little waiter. She placed the waiter on the top of her washing-stand, and seated herself on the bed, drawing Horace down beside her.

"My dear little grandson," said she, stroking his bright hair, "God has been very good to you always, always. He loves you better than you can even think."

"Yes, grandma," answered Horace, bewildered.

"He is your dear Father in heaven," she added, slowly. "He wants you to love him with all your heart, for now — you have no other father!"

Horace sprang up from the bed, his eyes wild with fear and surprise, yet having no idea what she meant.

"Why, my father's captain in the army! He's down South!"

"But have you never thought, dear, that he might be shot?"

"No, I never," cried Horace, running to

the window and back again in great excitement. "Mr. Evans said they'd put him in colonel. He was coming home in six months. He couldn't be shot!"

"My dear little boy!"

"But O, grandma, is he killed? Say quick!"

His grandmother took out of her pocket a Boston Journal, and having put on her spectacles, pointed with a trembling finger to the list of "killed." One of the first names was "Captain Henry S. Clifford."

"O, Horace!" said Grace, opening the door softly, "I just thought I heard you, Ma wants you to come to her."

Without speaking, Horace gave his hand to his sister, and went with her while their grandmother followed, carrying the bowl of gruel.

At the door of Mrs. Clifford's room they

met aunt Louise coming out. The sight of Horace and Grace walking tearfully, hand in hand, was very touching to her.

"You dear little fatherless children," she whispered, throwing her arms around them both, and dropping tears and kisses on their faces.

"O, I can't, I can't bear it," cried Grace; "my own dear papa, that I love best of any one in all the world!"

Horace ran to his mother, and throwing himself on the bed beside her, buried his face in the pillows.

"O, ma! I reckon 'tisn't true. It's another Captain Clifford."

His mother lay so very white and still that Horace drew away when he had touched her: there was something awful in the cold-ness of her face. Her beautiful brown eyes shone bright and tearless; but there were dark hollows under them, deep enough to hold many tears, if the time should ever come when she might shed them.

"O, little Horace," whispered she, "mother's little Horace!"

"Darling mamma!" responded the boy, kissing her pale lips and smoothing the hair away from her cheeks with his small fingers, which meant to move gently, but did not know how. And then the young, childish heart, with its little load of grief, was pressed close to the larger heart, whose deep, deep sorrow only God could heal.

They are wrong who say that little children cannot receive lasting impressions. There are some hours of joy or agony which they never forget. This was such an hour for Horace. He could almost feel again on his forehead the warm good-by kisses of his father; he could almost hear again the words —

"Always obey your mother, my son, and remember that God sees all you do."

Ah, he had not obeyed, he had not remembered.

And that dear father would never kiss him, never speak to him again! He had not thought before what a long word *Never* was.

O, it was dreadful to shut his eyes and fancy him lying so cold and still on that bloody battle-field! Would all this awful thing be true to-morrow morning, when he waked up?

"O, mamma," sobbed the desolate child, "I and Grace will take care of you! Just forgive me, ma, and I'll be the best kind of a boy. I will, I will!"

Grandma had already led Grace away into the green chamber, where aunt Madge sat with the baby. The poor little girl would not be comforted.

"O, grandma," she cried, " if we could know who it was that shot pa our mayor would hang him! I do wish I could die, grandma. I don't want to keep living and living in this great world without my father!"

9

CHAPTER IX.

THE BLUE BOOK.

Days passed, but there was the same hush upon the house. Everybody moved about softly, and spoke in low tones. Horace was not told that he must go to school, but he knew aunt Louise thought his shoes made a great deal of noise, and just now he wanted to please even her. More than that, it was very pleasant to see the boys; and while he was playing games he forgot his sorrow, and forgot his mother's sad face. There was one thing, however, which he could not do: he had not the heart to be captain, and drill his company, just now.

"Horace," said Grace, as they were sitting on the piazza steps one morning, "I heard ma tell grandma yesterday, you'd been a better boy this week than you had been before since — since — pa went away."

"Did she?" cried Horace, eagerly; "where was she when she said it? What did grandma say? Did aunt Madge hear her?"

"Yes, aunt Madge heard her, and she said she always knew Horace would be a good boy if he would only think."

"Well, I *do* think," replied Horace, looking very much pleased; "I think about all the time."

"But then, Horace, you know how you've acted some days!"

"Well, I don't care. Aunt Madge says 'tisn't so easy for boys to be good."

Grace opened her round blue eyes in wonder.

"Why, Horace, I have to make my own

bed, and sweep and dust my room, and take care of my drawers. Only think of that; and Prudy always round into things, you know! Then I have to sew, O, so much! I reckon you wouldn't find it very easy being a girl."

"Poh! don't I have to feed the chickens, and bring in the eggs, and go for the cows? And when we lived home —— "

Here Horace broke down; he could not think of home without remembering his father.

Grace burst into tears. The word "home" had called up a beautiful picture of her father and mother sitting on the sofa in the library, Horace and Pincher lying on the floor, the door open from the balcony, and the moon filling the room with a soft light: her father had a smile on his face, and was holding her hand.

Ah! Grace, and Horace, and their mother would see many such pictures of memory.

"Well, sister," said Horace, speaking quite slowly, and looking down at the grass, "what do I do that's bad?"

"Why, Horace, I shouldn't think you'd ask! Blowing gunpowder, and running off· into the woods, and most killing Pincher, and going trouting down to the 'crick' with your best clothes on, and disobeying your ma, and —— "

"Sayin' bad words," added Horace "but I stopped that this morning."

"What do you mean, Horace?"

"O, I said over all the bad things I could think of; not the swearin' words, you know, but 'shucks,' and 'gallus,' and 'bully,' and 'by hokey,' and 'by George;' and it's the last time."

"O, I'm so glad, Horace!" cried Grace,

clapping her hands and laughing; "and you won't blow any more powder?"

Horace shook his head.

"Nor run off again? Why, you'll be like Ally Glover, and you know I'm trying to be like little Eva."

"I don't want to be like Ally Glover," replied Horace, making a wry face; "he's lame, and besides, he's too dreadful good."

"Why, Horace," said his sister, solemnly; "anybody can't be too good; 'tisn't possible."

"Well, then, he's just like a girl — that's what! I'm not going to be 'characteristic' any more, but I don't want to be like a girl neither. Look here, Grace; it's school time. Now don't you 'let on' to ma, or anybody, that I'm going to be better."

Grace promised, but she wondered why Horace should not wish his mother to know he was trying to be good, when it would make her so happy.

CAPTAIN HORACE AND HIS DOG. *Page 138.*

"He's afraid he'll give it up," thought she; "but I won't let him."

She sat on the piazza steps a long while after he had gone. At last a bright idea flashed across her mind, and of course she dropped her work and clapped her hands, though she was quite alone.

"I'll make a merit-book like Miss All'n's, and put down black marks for him when he's naughty."

When Horace came home that night, he was charmed with the plan, for he was really in earnest. His kind sister made the book very neatly, and sewed it into a cover of glossy blue paper. She thought they would try it four weeks; so she had put in twenty-eight pages, each page standing for one day.

"Now," said she, "when you say one bad word I'll put down 'one B. W.' for short; but when you say two bad words, 'twill be 'two B. W.,' you know. When you blow gunpowder, that'll be ' B. G.'— no, 'B. G. P.,' for gunpowder is two words."

"And when I run off, 'twill be 'R. O.'"

"Or 'R. A.,' said Grace, for 'ran away.'"

"And 'T.' for 'troutin',' said Horace, who was getting very much interested; "and — and —'P. A. L.' for 'plaguing aunt Louise,' and 'C.' for 'characteristic,' and 'L. T.' for 'losing things.'"

"O, dear, dear, Horace, the book won't begin to hold it! We mustn't put down those little things."

"But, Grace, you know I shan't do 'em any more."

Grace shook her head, and sighed. "We won't put down all those little things," repeated she; "we'll have 'D.' for 'disobedience,' and 'B. W.,' and—O! one thing I forgot — 'F.' for 'falsehood.'"

"Well, you won't get any F's out of me, by hokey," said Horace, snapping his fingers.

"Why, there it is, 'one B. W.' *so* quick!" cried Grace, holding up both hands and laughing.

Horace opened his mouth in surprise, and then clapped his hand over it in dismay. It was not a very fortunate beginning.

"Look here, Grace," said he, making a wry face; "I move we call that no 'count, and commence new to-morrow!"

So Grace waited till next day before she dated the merit-book.

All this while Pincher's foot was growing no better. Aunt Louise said you could almost see the poor dog 'dwindle, peak, and pine.'"

"But it's only his hurt," said Grace: "'tisn't a sickness."

"I reckon," returned Horace, sadly, "it isn't a *wellness*, neither."

"Why not send for Mrs. Duffy?" suggested aunt Madge. "If any one can help the poor creature, it is she."

Mrs. Duffy was the village washerwoman, and a capital nurse. It was an anxious moment for little Horace, when she unwrapped the crushed paw, Pincher moaning all the while in a way that went to the heart.

"Wull," said Mrs. Duffy, who spoke with a brogue, "it's a bad-looking fut; but I've some intment here that'll do no har-rum, and it may hulp the poor craycher."

She put the salve on some clean linen cloths, and bound up the wound, bidding them all ne very careful that the dog "didn't stir his fut."

"O, but he don't want to stir!" said Horace. "He just lies down by the stove all day."

Mrs. Duffy shook her head, and said, "he was a pooty craycher; 'twas more the pities that he ever went off in the wuds."

Horace hung his head. O, if he could have blotted out that day of disobedience!

"Wasn't it a real rebel, *heathen* man," cried Prudy, "to put the trap where Pincher sticked his foot in it?"

Pincher grew worse and worse. He refused his food, and lay in a basket with a cushion in it, by the kitchen stove, where he might have been a little in the way, though not even aunt Louise ever said so.

If Grace, or Susy, or Prudy, went up to him, he made no sign. It was only when he saw his little master that he would wag his tail for joy; but even that effort seemed to tire him, and he liked better to lick Horace's hand, and look up at his face with eyes brimful of love and agony.

Horace would sit by the half hour, coaxing him to eat a bit of broiled steak or the wing of a chicken; but though the poor dog would gladly have pleased his young master, he could hardly force himself to swallow a mouthful.

These were sad days. Grace put down now and then a "B. W." in the blue book; but as for disobedience, Horace had just now no temptation to that. He could hardly think of anything but his dog.

Pincher was about his age. He could not remember the time when he first knew him. "O, what jolly times they had had together! How often Pincher had trotted along to school, carrying the satchel with the schoolbooks in his teeth. Why, the boys all loved him, they just loved him so."

"No, sir," said Horace, talking to himself, and laying the dog's head gently on his knee: "there wasn't one of them but just wished they had him. But, poh! I wouldn't have sold him for all the cannons and fire-crackers in the United States. No, not for a real drum, either; would I, Pincher?"

Horace really believed the dog understood him, and many were the secrets he had poured into his faithful ears. Pincher would listen, and wink, and wag his tail, but was sure to keep everything to himself.

"I tell you what it is, Pincher," Horace burst forth, "I'm not going to have you die! My own pa gave you to me, and you're the best dog that ever lived in this world. O, I didn't mean to catch your foot in that trap! Eat the chicken, there's a good fellow, and we'll cure you all up."

But Pincher couldn't eat the chicken, and couldn't be cured. His eyes grew larger and sadder, but there was the same patient look in them always. He fixed them on Horace to the last, with a dying gaze which made the boy's heart swell with bitter sorrow.

" He wanted to speak, he wanted to ask me a question," said Horace, with sobs he did not try to control.

O, it was sad to close those beautiful eyes forever, those beseeching eyes, which could almost speak.

Mrs. Clifford came and knelt on the stone hearth beside the basket, and wept freely for the first time since her husband's death.

" Dear little Pincher," said she, " you have died a cruel death; but your dear little master closed your eyes. It was very hard, poor doggie, but not so hard as the battle-field. You shall have a quiet grave, good Pincher; but where have they buried our brave soldier? "

CHAPTER X.

TRYING TO GET RICH.

WITH his own hands, and the help of Grasshopper, who did little but hold the nails and look on, Horace made a box for Pincher, while Abner dug his grave under a tree in the grove.

It was evening when they all followed Pincher to his last resting-place.

"He was a sugar-plum of a dog," said Prudy, "and I can't help crying."

"I don't want to help it," said Grace: "we ought to cry."

"What makes me feel the worst," said sober little Susy, "he won't go to heaven."

"Not forever'n ever amen?" gasped
Prudy, in a low voice: "wouldn't he if he
had a nice casket, and a plate on it neither?"

The sky and earth were very lovely that
evening, and it seemed as if everybody
ought to be heart-glad. I doubt if Horace
had ever thought before what a beautiful
world he lived in, and how glorious a thing
it is to be alive! He could run about and
do what he pleased with himself; but alas,
poor Pincher!

The sun was setting, and the river looked
uncommonly full of little sparkles. The
soft sky, and the twinkling water, seemed to
be smiling at each other, while a great way
off you could see the dim blue mountains
rising up like clouds. Such a lovely world!
Ah! poor Pincher.

It looked very much as if Horace were
really turning over a new leaf. He was still

quite trying sometimes, leaving the milk-room door open when puss was watching for the cream-pot, or slamming the kitchen door with a bang when everybody needed fresh air. He still kept his chamber in a state of confusion, — "muss," Grace called it, — pulling the drawers out of the bureau, and scattering the contents over the floor; dropping his clothes anywhere it happened, and carrying quantities of gravel up stairs in his shoes.

Aunt Louise still scolded about him; but even she could not help seeing that on the whole he was improving. He "cared" more and "forgot" less. He could always learn easily, and now he really tried to learn. His lessons, instead of going through his head "threading my grandmother's needle," went in and staid there. The blue book got a few marks, it is true, but not so many as at first.

You may be sure there was not a good thing said or done by Horace which did not give pleasure to his mother. She felt now as if she lived only for her children; if God would bless her by making them good, she had nothing more to desire. Grace had always been a womanly, thoughtful little girl, but at this time she was a greater comfort than ever; and Horace had grown so tender and affectionate, that it gratified her very much. He was not content now with "canary kisses;" but threw his arms around her neck very often, saying, with his lips close to her cheek, —

"Don't feel bad, ma: I'm going to take care of you."

For his mother's grief called forth his manliness.

She meant to be cheerful: but Horace knew she did not look or seem like herself:

he thought he ought to try to make her happy.

Whenever he asked for money, as he too often did, she told him that now his father was gone, there was no one to earn anything, and it was best to be rather prudent. He wanted a drum; but she thought he must wait a while for that.

They were far from being poor, and Mrs. Clifford had no idea of deceiving her little son. Yet he *was* deceived, for he supposed that his mother's pretty little porte-monnaie held all the bank-bills and all the silver she had in the world.

"O, Grace!" said Horace, coming down stairs with a very grave face, "I wish I was grown a man: then I'd earn money like sixty."

Grace stopped her singing long enough to

ask what he meant to do, and then continued in a high key, —

"Where, O where are the Hebrew children?"

"O, I'm going as a soldier," replied Horace: "I thought everybody knew that! The colonels make a heap of money!"

"But, Horace, you might get shot — just think!"

"Then I'd dodge when they fired, for I don't know what you and ma would do if *I* was killed."

"Well, please step out of the way, Horace; don't you see I'm sweeping the piazza?"

"I can't tell," pursued he, taking a seat on one of the stairs in the hall: "I can't tell certain sure; but I may be a minister."

This was such a funny idea, that Grace made a dash with her broom, and sent the dirt flying the wrong way.

"Why, Horace, you'll never be good enough for a minister!"

"What'll you bet?" replied he, looking a little mortified.

"You're getting to be a dear good little boy, Horace," said Grace, soothingly; "but I don't *think* you'll ever be a minister."

"Perhaps I'd as soon be a shoemaker," continued Horace, thoughtfully; "they get a great deal for tappin' boots."

His sister made no reply.

"See here, now, Grace: perhaps you'd rather I'd be a tin-pedler; then I'd always keep a horse, and you could ride."

"Ride in a cart!" cried Grace, laughing. "Can't you think of anything else? Have you forgotten papa?"

"O, now I know," exclaimed Horace, with shining eyes: "it's a lawyer I'll be, just like father was. I'll have a 'sleepy partner,' the way Judge Ingle has, and by and by I'll be a judge."

"I know that would please ma, Horace," replied Grace, looking at her little brother with a good deal of pride.

Who knew but he *might* yet be a judge? She liked to order him about, and have him yield to her: still she had great faith in Horace.

" But, Grace, after all that I'll go to war, and turn out a general; now you see if I don't."

"That'll be a great while yet," said Grace, sighing.

" So it will," replied Horace, sadly; "and ma needs the money now. I wish I could earn something right off while I'm a little boy."

It was not two days before he thought he had found out how to get rich; in what way you shall see.

CHAPTER XI.

THE LITTLE INDIAN.

PRUDY came into the house one day in a great fright, and said they'd "better hide the baby, for there was a very wicked woman round."

"Her hair looks like a horse's tail," said she, "and she's got a black man's hat on her head, and a table-cloth over her."

Aunt Madge took Prudy in her lap, and told her it was only an Indian woman, who uad no idea of harming any one.

"What are Nindians?" asked the child.

Her aunt said they were sometimes called "red men." The country had once been filled by them: but the English came, a great many years ago, and shook off the red men just as a high wind shakes the red leaves off a tree; and they were scattered about, and only a few were left alive. Sometimes the Oldtown Indians came round making baskets; but they were quiet and peaceable people.

Horace and his friend "Grasshopper," as they were strolling up the river, came upon a tent made of canvas, and at the door of the tent sat a little boy about their own age, with a bow and arrow in his hand, in the act of firing.

Grasshopper, who was always a coward, ran with all his might; but as Horace happened to notice that the arrow was pointed at something across the river, he was not alarmed, but stopped to look at the odd little stranger, who turned partly round and returned his gaze. His eyes were keen and black, with a good-natured expression, something like the eyes of an intelligent dog.

"What's your name, boy?" said Horace.

"Me no understand."

"I asked what your *name* is," continued Horace, who was sure the boy understood, in spite of his blank looks.

"Me no hurt white folks; me bunkum Indian."

"Well, what's your name, then? What do they call you?"

No answer, but a shake of the head.

"I reckon they call you *John*, don't they?"

Here the boy's mother appeared at the door.

"His name no *John!* Eshy-ishy-oshy-neeshy - George - Wampum - Shoony - Katoo ! short name, speak um quick ! — Jaw-awn ! Great long name !" drawled she, stretching it out as if it were made of India rubber, and scowling with an air of disgust.

"What does she mean by calling 'John' *long?*" thought Horace.

The woman wore a calico dress, short enough to reveal her brown, stockingless feet and gay moccasons.

Her hair was crow-black, and strayed over her shoulders and into her eyes. Horace concluded she must have lost her back-comb.

While he was looking at her with curious eyes, her daughter came to the door, feeling a little cross at the stranger, whoever it might be; but when she saw only an innocent little boy, she smiled pleasantly, showing a row of white teeth. Horace thought her rather handsome, for she was very straight and slender, and her eyes shone like glass beads. Her hair he considered a great deal blacker than black, and it was braided and tied with gay red ribbons. She was dressed in a bright, large-figured calico, and from her ears were suspended the longest, yellowest, queerest, ear-rings. Horace thought they were shaped like boat-paddles, and would be pretty for Prudy to use when she rowed her little red boat in the bathing-tub. If they only "scooped" a little more they would answer for tea-spoons. "Plenty big as I should want for tea-spoons," he decided, after another gaze at them.

The young girl was used to being admired by her own people, and was not at all displeased with Horace for staring at her.

"Me think you nice white child," said she: "you get me sticks, me make you basket, pretty basket for put apples in."

"What kind of sticks do you mean?" said Horace, forgetting that they pretended

not to understand English. But it appeared
that they knew very well what he meant this
time, and the Indian boy offered to go with
him to point out the place where the wood
was to be found. Grasshopper, who had
only hidden behind the trees, now came out
and joined the boys.

"Wampum," as he chose to be called, led
them back to Mr. Parlin's grounds, to the
lower end of the garden, where stood some
tall silver poplars, on which the Indians had
looked with longing eyes.

"Me shin them trees," said Wampum;
"me make you basket."

"Would you let him, Grasshopper?"

"Yes, indeed; your grandfather won't
care."

"Perhaps he might; you don't know,"
said Horace, who, after he had asked advice,
was far from feeling obliged to take it. He

ran in great haste to the field where his grandfather was hoeing potatoes, thinking, "If I ask, then I shan't get marked in the blue book anyhow."

In this case Horace acted very properly. He had no right to cut the trees, or allow any one else to cut them, without leave. To his great delight, his grandfather said he did not care if they clipped off a few branches where they would not show much.

When Horace got back and reported the words of his grandfather, Wampum did not even smile, but shot a glance at him as keen as an arrow.

"Me no hurt trees," said he, gravely; and he did not: he only cut off a few limbs from each one, leaving the trees as handsome as ever.

"Bully for you!" cried Horace, forgetting the blue book.

"He's as spry as a squirrel," said Grass·hopper, in admiration; "how many boughs has he got? One, two, three."

"Me say 'em quickest," cried little Wampum. "Een, teen, teddery, peddery, bimp, satter, latter, doe, dommy, dick."

"That's ten," put in Horace, who was keeping 'count.

"Een-dick," continued the little Indian, "teen-dick, teddery-dick, peddery-dick, bumpin, een-bumpin, teen-bumpin, teddery-bumpin, peddery-bumpin, jiggets."

"Hollo!" cried Grasshopper; "that's twenty; jiggets is twenty;" and he rolled over on the ground, laughing as if he had made a great discovery.

Little by little they made Wampum tell how he lived at home, what sort of boys he played with, and what they had to eat. The young Indian assured them that at Oldtown "he lived in a house good as white folks; he ate moose-meat, ate sheep-meat, ate cow-meat."

"Cook out doors, I s'pose," said Grasshopper.

Wampum looked very severe. "When me lives in wigwam, me has fires in wigwam: when me lives in tent, me puts fires on grass;—keep off them things," he added, pointing at a mosquito in the air; "keep smoke out tent," pointing upward to show the motion of the smoke.

Horace felt so much pleased with his new companion, that he resolved to treat him to a watermelon. So, without saying a word to the boys, he ran into the house to ask his grandmother.

"What! a whole watermelon, Horace?"

"Yes, grandma, we three; me, and Grasshopper, and Wampum."

Mrs. Parlin could not help smiling to see how suddenly Horace had adopted a new friend.

"You may have a melon, but I think your mother would not like to have you play much with a strange boy."

"He's going to make me a splendid basket; and besides, aren't Indians and negroes as good as white folks? 'Specially *tame* Indians," said Horace, not very respectfully, as he ran back, shoe-knife in hand, to cut the watermelon.

This was the beginning of a hasty friendship between himself and Wampum. For a few days there was nothing so charming to Horace as the wild life of this Indian family. He was made welcome at their tent, and often went in to see them make baskets.

"I trust you," said Mrs. Clifford; "you will not deceive me, Horace. If you ever find that little Wampum says bad words, tells falsehoods, or steals, I shall not be willing for you to play with him. You are very young, and might be greatly injured by bad playmate."

The tent was rude enough. In one corner were skins laid one over another : these were the beds which were spread out at night for the family. Instead of closets and presses, all the wearing apparel was hung on a long rope, which was stretched from stake to stake, in various directions, like a clothesline.

It was curious to watch the brown fingers moving so easily over the white strips, out of which they wove baskets. It was such pretty work! it brought so much money. Horace thought it was just the business for him, and Wampum promised to teach him. In return for this favor, Horace was to instruct the little Indian in spelling.

For one or two evenings he appointed meetings in the summer-house, and really went without his own slice of cake, that he might give it to poor Wampum, after a lesson in " baker."

He received the basket in due time, a beautiful one — red, white, and blue. Just as he was carrying it home on his arm, he met Billy Green, the hostler, who stopped him, and asked if he remembered going into " the Pines " one day with Peter Grant? Horace had no reason to forget it, surely.

" Seems to me you ran away with my horse-basket," said Billy; " but I never knew till yesterday what had 'come of it."

" There, now," replied Horace, quite crest-fallen; " Peter Grant took that! I forgot all about it."

What should be done? It would never do to ask his mother for the money, since as he believed, she had none to spare. Billy was fond of joking with little boys.

"Look here, my fine fellow," said he, "give us that painted concern you've got on your arm, and we'll call it square."

"No, no, Billy," cried Horace, drawing away; "this is a present, and I couldn't. But I'm learning to weave baskets, and I'll make you one — see if I don't!"

Billy laughed, and went away whistling. He had no idea that Horace would ever think of the matter again; but in truth the first article the boy tried to make was a horse-basket.

"Me tell you somethin," said little Wampum, next morning, as he and Horace were crossing the field together. "Very much me want um, — um, — um," — putting his fingers up to his mouth in a manner which signified that he meant something to eat.

"Don't understand," said Horace: "say it in English."

"Very much me want um," continued Wampum, in a beseeching tone. "No tell what you call um. E'enamost water, no *quite* water; e'enamost punkin, no *quite* punkin."

"Poh! you mean watermelon," laughed Horace: "should think you'd remember that as easy as pumpkin."

"Very much me want um," repeated Wampum, delighted at being understood; "me like um."

"Well," replied Horace, "they aren't mine."

"O, yes. Ugh! you've got 'em. Melon-water good! Me have melon-waters, me give you moc-suns."

"I'll ask my grandpa, Wampum."

Hereupon the crafty little Indian shook his head.

"You ask ole man, me no give you moc-suns! Me no want *een* — me want bimp — bumpin — jiggets."

Horace's stout little heart wavered for a moment. He fancied moccasins very much. In his mind's eye he saw a pair shining with all the colors of the rainbow, and as Wam-pum had said of the melons, "very much he wanted them." How handsome they'd be with his Zouave suit!

But the wavering did not last long. He remembered the blue book which his mother was to see next week; for then the month would be out.

"It wouldn't be a 'D.,'" thought he, "for nobody told me *not* to give the water-melons."

"No," said Conscience; "'twould be a black S.; *that* stands for stealing! What, a boy with a dead father, a dead soldier-father, *steal!*   A boy called Horace Clifford! The boy whose father had said, 'Remember God sees all you do!'"

"Wampum," said Horace, firmly, "you just stop that kind of talk! Moccasins are right pretty; but I wouldn't steal, no, not if you gave me a bushel of 'em."

After this, Horace was disgusted with his little friend, not remembering that there are a great many excuses to be made for a half-civilized child. They had a serious quarrel, and Wampum's temper proved to be very bad. If the little savage had not struck him, I hope Horace would have dropped his society all the same; because, after Wampum proved to be a thief, it would have been sheer disobedience on Horace's part to play with him any longer.

Of course the plan of basket-making was given up; but our little Horace did one thing which was noble in a boy of his age: perhaps he remembered what his father had said long ago in regard to the injured watch; but, at any rate, he went to Billy Green of his own accord, and offered him the beautiful present which he had received from the Indians.

"It's not a horse-basket, Billy: I didn't get to make one," stammered he, in a choked voice; "but you said you'd call it square."

"Whew!" cried Billy, very much astonished: "now look here, bub; that's a little too bad! The old thing you lugged off was about worn out, anyhow. Don't want any of your fancy baskets: so just carry it back, my fine little shaver."

To say that Horace was very happy, would not half express the delight he felt as he ran home with the beautiful basket on his arm, his "ownest own," beyond the right of dispute.

The Indians disappeared quite suddenly; and perhaps it was nothing surprising that, the very next morning after they left, grandpa Parlin should find his beautiful melon-patch stripped nearly bare, with nothing left on the vines but a few miserable green little melons.

CHAPTER XII.

A PLEASANT SURPRISE.

"It's too bad," said Horace to his sister, "that I didn't get to make baskets; I'd have grown rich so soon. What would you try to do next?"

"Pick berries," suggested Grace.

And that very afternoon they both went blackberrying with Susy and aunt Madge. They had a delightful time. Horace could not help missing Pincher very much: still, in spite of the regret, it was a happier day than the one he and Peter Grant had spent "in the Pines." He was beginning to find, as all children do, how hard it is to get up "a good time" when you are pricked by a guilty conscience, and how easy it is to be happy when you are doing right.

They did not leave the woods till the sun began to sink, and reached home quite tired, but as merry as larks, with baskets nearly full of berries.

When Horace timidly told aunt Madge that he and Grace wanted to sell all they had gathered, his aunt laughed, and said she would buy the fruit if they wished, but wondered what they wanted to do with the money: she supposed it was for the soldiers.

"I want to give it to ma," replied Horace, in a low voice; for he did not wish his aunt Louise to overhear. "She hasn't more than three bills in her pocket-book, and it's time for me to begin to take care of her."

"Ah," said aunt Madge, with one of her bright smiles, "there is a secret drawer in her writing-desk, dear, that has ever so much money in it. She isn't poor, my child, and she didn't mean to make you think so, for your mother wouldn't deceive you."

"Not poor?" cried Horace, his face brightening suddenly; and he turned half a somerset, stopping in the midst of it to ask how much a drum would cost.

The month being now out, it was time to show the blue book to Mrs. Clifford. Horace looked it over with some anxiety. On each page were the letters "D.," "B. W.," "B. G. P.," and "F.," on separate lines, one above another. But there were no figures before any of the letters but the "B. W.'s;" and even those figures had been growing rather smaller, as you could see by looking carefully.

"Now, Grace," said her little brother,

"you'll tell ma that the bad words aren't swearin' words! I never did say such, though some of the fellows do, and those that go to Sabbath School too."

"Yes, I'll tell her," said Grace; "but she knows well enough that you never talk anything worse than lingo."

"I haven't disobeyed, nor blown powder, nor told lies."

"No, indeed," said Grace, delighted. "To be sure, you've forgotten, and slammed doors, and lost things; but you know I didn't set that down."

I wish all little girls felt as much interest in their younger brothers as this sister felt in Horace. Grace had her faults, of which I might have told you if I had been writing the book about her; but she loved Horace dearly, kept his little secrets whenever she promised to do so, and was always glad to have him do right.

Mrs. Clifford was pleased with the idea of the blue book, and kissed Horace and Grace, saying they grew dearer to her every day of their lives.

One night, not long after this, Horace went to the post-office for the mail. This was nothing new, for he had often gone before. A crowd of men were sitting in chairs and on the door-stone and counter, listening to the news, which some one was reading in a loud, clear voice.

Without speaking, the postmaster gave Horace three letters and a newspaper. After tucking the letters into his raglan pocket, Horace rolled the paper into a hollow tube, peeping through it at the large tree standing opposite the post-office, and at the patient horses hitched to the posts, waiting for their masters to come out.

He listened for some time to the dreadful account of a late battle, thinking of his dear father, as he always did when he heard war-news. But at last remembering that his grandfather would be anxious to have the daily paper, he started for home, though rather against his will.

"I never did see such a fuss as they make," thought he, "if anybody's more'n a minute going to the office and back."

"Is this all?" said aunt Madge, as Horace gave a letter to grandma, one to aunt Louise, and the paper to his grandfather.

"Why, yes, ma'am, that's all," replied Horace, faintly. It did seem, to be sure, as if Mr. Pope had given him three letters; but as he could not find another in his pocket, he supposed he must be mistaken, and said nothing about it. He little knew what a careless thing he had done, and soon went to bed, forgetting post-offices and letters in a strange dream of little Wampum, who had a bridle on and was hitched to a post; and of the Indian girl's ear-rings, which seemed to have grown into a pair of shining gold muskets.

A few mornings after the mistake about the letter, Mrs. Clifford sat mending Horace's raglan. She emptied the pockets of twine, fish-hooks, jack-knife, pebbles, coppers, and nails; but still something rattled when she touched the jacket; it seemed to be paper. She thrust in her finger, and there, between the outside and lining, was a crumpled, worn letter, addressed to "Miss Margaret Parlin."

"What does this mean?" thought Mrs. Clifford. "Horace must have carried the letter all summer."

But upon looking at it again, she saw that

it was mailed at Washington about two weeks before — "a soldier's letter." She carried it down to Margaret, who was busy making cream-cakes.

"Let me see," said aunt Louise, peeping over Mrs. Clifford's shoulder, and laughing. "No, it's not Mr. Augustus Allen's writing; but how do you know somebody hasn't written it to tell you he is sick?"

Aunt Madge grew quite pale, dropped the egg-beater, and carried the letter into the nursery to read it by herself. She opened it with trembling fingers; but before she had read two lines her fingers trembled worse than ever, her heart throbbed fast, the room seemed to reel about.

There was no bad news in the letter, you may be sure of that. She sat reading it over and over again, while the tears ran down her cheeks, and the sunshine in her eyes dried them again. Then she folded her hands together, and humbly thanked God for his loving kindness.

When she was sure her sister Maria had gone up stairs, she ran out to the kitchen, whispering, —

"O, mother! O, Louise!" but broke down by laughing.

"What does ail the child?" said Mrs. Parlin, laughing too.

Margaret tried again to speak, but this time burst into tears.

"There, it's of no use," she sobbed: "I'm so happy that it's really dreadful. I'm afraid somebody may die of joy."

"I'm more afraid somebody'll die of curiosity," said aunt Louise: "do speak quick."

"Well, Henry Clifford is alive," said Margaret: "that's the blessed truth! Now hush! We must be so careful how we tell Maria!"

Mrs. Parlin caught Margaret by the shoulder, and gasped for breath. Louise dropped into a chair.

"What do you mean? What have you heard?" they both cried at once.

"He was taken off the field for dead; but life was not quite gone. He lay for weeks just breathing, and that was all."

"But why did no one let us know it?" said Louise. "Of course Maria would have gone to him at once."

"There was no one to write; and when Henry came to himself there was no hope of him, except by amputation of his left arm; and after that operation he was very low again."

"O, why don't you give us the letter." said Louise, "so we can see for ourselves?"

But she was too excited to read it: and while she was trying to collect her ideas, aunt Madge had to hunt for grandma's spectacles; and then the three looked over the surgeon's letter together, sometimes all talking at once.

Captain Clifford would be in Maine as soon as possible: so the letter said. A young man was to come with him to take care of him, and they were to travel very slowly indeed; might be at home in a fortnight.

"They may be here to-night," said Mrs. Parlin.

This letter had been written to prepare the family for Captain Clifford's arrival. It was expected that aunt Madge would break the news to his wife.

"It's such a pity that little flyaway of a Horace didn't give you the letter in time," said Louise; "and then we might have had some days to get used to it."

"Wait a minute, dear," said aunt Madge, as Susy came in for a drink of water: "please run up and ask aunt Maria to come down stairs. Now, mother," she added, "you are the one to tell the story, if you please."

"We can all break it to her by degrees," said Mrs. Parlin, twisting her checked apron nervously.

When Mrs. Clifford entered the kitchen, she saw at once that something had happened. Her mother, with a flushed face, was opening and shutting the stove door. Margaret was polishing a pie-plate, with tears in her eyes, and Louise had seized a sieve, and appeared to be breaking eggs into it. Nobody wanted to speak first.

"What do you say to hearing a story?" fluttered Louise.

"O, you poor woman," exclaimed Margaret, seizing Mrs. Clifford by both hands : "you look so sorrowful, dear, as if nothing would ever make you happy again. Can you believe we have a piece of good news for you?"

"For me?" Mrs. Clifford looked bewildered.

"Good news for you," said Louise, dropping the sieve to the floor: "yes, indeed! O, Maria, we thought Henry was killed; but he isn't; it's a mistake of the papers. He's alive, and coming home to-night."

All this as fast as she could speak. No wonder Mrs. Clifford was shocked! First she stood quiet and amazed, gazing at her sister with fixed eyes: then she screamed, and would have fallen if her mother and Margaret had not caught her in their arms.

"O, I have killed her," cried Louise : "I didn't mean to speak so quick! Henry is *almost* dead, Maria: he is *nearly* dead, I mean! He's just alive!"

"Louise, bring some water at once," said Mrs. Parlin, sternly.

"O, mother," sobbed Louise, returning with the water, "I didn't mean to be so hasty; but you might have known I would: you should have sent me out of the room."

This was very much the way Prudy talked when she did wrong: she had a funny way of blaming other people.

It is always unsafe to tell even joyful news too suddenly; but Louise's thoughtlessness had not done so much harm as they all feared. Mrs. Clifford recovered from the shock, and in an hour or two was wonderfully calm, looking so perfectly happy that it was delightful just to gaze at her face.

She wanted the pleasure of telling the

children the story with her own lips. Grace was fairly wild with joy, kissing everybody, and declaring it was "too good for anything." She was too happy to keep still, while as for Horace, he was too happy to talk.

" Then uncle Henry wasn't gone to heaven," cried little Prudy : " hasn't he been to heaven at all?"

"No, of course not," said Susy : "didn't you hear 'em say he'd be here to-night? — Now you've got on the nicest kind of a dress, and if you spot it up 'twill be awful."

"I guess," pursued Prudy, "the man that shooted found 'twas uncle Henry, and so he didn't want to kill him down dead."

How the family found time to do so many things that day, I do not know, especially as each one was in somebody's way, and the children under everybody's feet. But before night the pantry was full of nice things, the whole house was as fresh as a rose, and the parlors were adorned with autumn flowers and green garlands.

Not only the kerosene lamps, but all the old oil lamps, were filled, and every candle-stick, whether brass, iron, or glass, was used to hold a sperm candle; so that in the evening the house at every window was all ablaze with light. The front door stood wide open, and the piazza and part of the lawn were as bright as day. The double gate had been unlatched for hours, and everybody was waiting for the carriage to drive up.

The hard, uncomfortable stage, which Horace had said was like a baby-jumper, would never do for a sick man to ride in: so Billy Green had driven to the cars in his easiest carriage, and aunt Madge had gone with him, for she was afraid neither Billy nor the gentleman who was with Captain Clifford would know how to wrap the shawls about him carefully enough.

I could never describe the joyful meeting which took place in those brilliantly lighted parlors. It is very rarely that such wonderful happiness falls to any one's lot in this world.

While the smiles are yet bright on their faces, while Grace is clinging to her father's neck, and Horace hugs his new "real drum" in one arm, embracing his dear papa with the other, let us take our leave of them and the whole family for the present, with many kind good-by's.

✠ SOPHIE ✠ MAY'S ✠

"LITTLE-FOLKS" BOOKS.

"THE authoress of THE LITTLE PRUDY STORIES would be elected Aunty-laureate if the children had an opportunity, for the wonderful books she writes for their amusement. She is the Dickens of the nursery, and we do not hesitate to say develops the rarest sort of genius in the specialty of depicting smart little children." — *Hartford Post.*

LEE AND SHEPARD, PUBLISHERS, BOSTON.

"The children will not be left without healthful entertainment and kindly instruction so long as SOPHIE MAY (Miss Rebecca S. Clarke) lives and wields her graceful pen in their behalf. Miss CLARKE has made a close and loving study of childhood, and she is almost idolized by the crowd of 'nephews and nieces' who claim her as aunt. Nothing to us can ever be quite so delightfully charming as were the 'Dotty Dimple' and the 'Little Prudy' books to our youthful imagination; but we have no doubt the little folks of to-day will find the story of 'Flaxie Frizzle' and her young friends just as fascinating. There is a sprightliness about all of Miss CLARKE's books that attracts the young, and their purity, their absolute *cleanliness*, renders them invaluable in the eyes of parents and all who are interested in the welfare of children." — *Morning Star*.

"Genius comes in with 'Little Prudy.' Compared with her, all other book-children are cold creations of literature; she alone is the real thing. All the quaintness of children, its originality, its tenderness and its teasing, its infinite uncommon drollery, the serious earnestness of its fun, the fun of its seriousness, the naturalness of its plays, and the delicious oddity of its progress, all these united for dear Little Prudy to embody them." — *North American Review*.

Illustrated. Comprising:—

LITTLE PRUDY.
LITTLE PRUDY'S SISTER SUSIE.
LITTLE PRUDY'S CAPTAIN HORACE.
LITTLE PRUDY'S COUSIN GRACE.
LITTLE PRUDY'S STORY BOOK.
LITTLE PRUDY'S DOTTY DIMPLE.

In neat box. Price 75 cents per volume.

LITTLE PRUDY.

"I have been wanting to say a word about a book for children, perfect of its kind—I mean LITTLE PRUDY. It seems to me the greatest book of the season for children. The authoress has a genius for story-telling. Prudy's letter to Mr. 'Gustus Somebody must be genuine; if an invention, it shows a genius akin to that of the great masters. It is a positive kindness to the little ones to remind their parents that there is such a book as LITTLE PRUDY."—*Springfield Republican.*

LITTLE PRUDY'S SISTER SUSIE.

"Every little girl and boy who has made the acquaintance of that funny 'Little Prudy' will be eager to read this book, in which she figures quite as largely as her bigger sister, though the joys and troubles of poor Susie make a very interesting story."—*Portland Transcript.*

"Certainly one of the most cunning, natural, and witty little books we ever read."—*Hartford Press.*

LITTLE PRUDY'S CAPTAIN HORACE.

"These are such as none but SOPHIE MAY can write, and we know not where to look for two more choice and beautiful volumes—SUSIE for girls and HORACE for boys. They are not only amusing and wonderfully entertaining, but teach most effective lessons of patience, kindness, and truthfulness. Our readers will find a good deal in them about Prudy, for so many things are always happening to her that the author finds it impossible to keep her out."

www.ingramcontent.com/pod-product-compliance
Lightning Source LLC
Chambersburg PA
CBHW020620030726
47497CB00007B/2341